Gustavus D Pike

**The Singing Campaign for Ten Thousand Pounds**

Or, the Jubilee Singers in Great Britain; with an appendix containing slave songs

Gustavus D Pike

**The Singing Campaign for Ten Thousand Pounds**
*Or, the Jubilee Singers in Great Britain; with an appendix containing slave songs*

ISBN/EAN: 9783337410216

Printed in Europe, USA, Canada, Australia, Japan

Cover: Foto ©Thomas Meinert / pixelio.de

More available books at **www.hansebooks.com**

# THE SINGING CAMPAIGN

FOR

## TEN THOUSAND POUNDS;

OR,

## THE JUBILEE SINGERS IN GREAT BRITAIN.

BY THE

REV. GUSTAVUS D. PIKE.

WITH AN

APPENDIX CONTAINING SLAVE SONGS.

*REVISED EDITION.*

FOR SALE BY THE
AMERICAN MISSIONARY ASSOCIATION,
56 READE STREET, NEW YORK.
1875.

Entered, according to Act of Congress, in the year 1875, by
THE AMERICAN MISSIONARY ASSOCIATION,
in the Office of the Librarian of Congress, at Washington.

TO THE

RIGHT HON. THE EARL OF SHAFTESBURY, K.G.,

OF ENGLAND,

AND

THE HON. GEO. H. STUART,

OF AMERICA,

AS AN HUMBLE TOKEN OF THEIR NOBLE PHILANTHROPY

IN BEHALF OF THE JUBILEE SINGERS,

AND THE RACE THEY REPRESENT,

THIS VOLUME IS MOST GRATEFULLY INSCRIBED

BY

THE AUTHOR.

# PREFACE TO AMERICAN EDITION.

A PREVIOUS volume narrated the history of the campaign of the Jubilee Singers in America: this gives their experiences in Great Britain. Their reception there was so remarkable, and their success so great, that the simple details seem to be all that is needed. The episodes introduced as conversations with a friend are not foreign to the subject, but are intended to show withal the intimate relations between the Christian education of the Freedmen and the evangelization of Africa.

The introduction was kindly furnished by Rev. E. M. Cravath, Field Secretary of the American Missionary Association, one of the founders of Fisk University.

One of the plates prefixed to the volume gives the portraits of the Singers with the names designated beneath, and the other plate represents Jubilee Hall, Nashville, Tenn.

Appended to the book are the slave songs sung by the Jubilee Singers, including a number of pieces never heretofore published.

G. D. P.

56 Reade St., New York, March 1, 1875.

# INTRODUCTION.

The Jubilee Singers are students of a University whose founding was connected with the close of the war and the opening of the great effort for the Christian elevation of the Freedmen.

In June 1865, Maj. Gen. Geo. H. Thomas held the grand review of his victorious army of veterans which he had concentrated at Nashville, when the war ended, preparatory to mustering them out of service. One of the large hospital buildings in that city, from which the sick and wounded soldiers of the retiring army were withdrawn, became soon afterwards a fountain of life, light and inspiration to the struggling Freedmen.

The officers' quarters became the home of an earnest band of Christian teachers; the sick wards, which had been left empty by the return of the soldiers to their homes and friends, became school-rooms for hundreds of eager children; and the dead-house became the store-room of supplies for the naked and suffering.

In the October following the retiring of the army, the half block of land and the hospital thereon were purchased for the purpose of establishing a Christian school for the education of the Freedmen—and it is a notable fact that the four men who were personally connected with the work the first year, had all been in service with the army, in the department of which Nashville was the base of operations.

The formal opening of the school took place January 1866, and from the very first, the pupils and the public were informed that the Institution had been founded with a view to permanence, and that it would provide for the most advanced wants of those who should seek its advantages, until regular collegiate and professional training should be given.

Without question this was the first institution established in the South for the Freedmen with this distinct and avowed purpose. During the six years from its beginning to the departure of the Jubilee Singers, uninterrupted prosperity was enjoyed. The catalogue of 1870–71 gave the number of different pupils in attendance during the year as 477, and at the Annual Commencement of that year the Collegiate Department was organized by the entering of a Freshman class of four.

But with all this success there had been this constantly increasing occasion of anxiety: the site and buildings which were admirably adapted to the work of the first few years, were entirely unsuited to the permanent uses of the Institution. The grounds were limited, and too central in the city, and the slight frame buildings were fast going to decay. A commanding site near the city, ample for the future of a great university must soon be purchased, and permanent buildings erected. The raising of the large sum of money required for this purpose must be provided for. At the close of the school in 1871, it was felt that the time had come when in some way the effort must at once be made. The question anxiously asked, How shall this be done? was answered by a proposition from Geo. L. White, the Treasurer, to undertake this work by giving concerts with a band of Singers selected from among the students. Mr. White had become connected with the school at its opening—being then in Government employ in the city—by voluntarily offering to give without compensation a part of each day to the teaching of vocal music. In his subsequent and permanent connection with the institution he had organized a large choir of singers, from whom he proposed to select a band whose gift of song had been developed incidentally, and to use it, to save in the time of its necessity, the institution that had sheltered and instructed them.

The plan being approved by the Trustees, the company was selected and the summer spent in special training and preparation. They did not propose to appear before the public as professional musicians: the time had been too short and opportunities for culture too limited for them to compete with those who through the aid of the labor and study of centuries had brought music to its present state of perfection. Instead of this they interpreted the spiritual and religious power of the songs of the slaves of the South, and thus touched the hearts of the Christian people everywhere and secured their sympathy and liberal aid.

The Singers left Fisk University October 1871 and returned in time to attend the Commencement exercises the last of May 1874; having given two seasons of concerts in the United States and one in Great Britain. The history of the heroic struggles of the first three months and of the marvelous success of the remaining four months of their first year, has been published in the book entitled "The Jubilee Singers and their campaign for Twenty Thousand Dollars," more than 30,000 copies of which have been sold in the United States and Great Britain. The sketch of the Campaign in Great Britain, with its remarkable providential openings and triumphant results, is given in the volume now in the reader's hands: the net result of the three years was $90,000, with which the permanent site of twenty-five acres has been purchased and Jubilee Hall nearly completed.

The University is in pressing need of another building, and of an endowment for the support of its professors. Up to the present time, the sums raised by the Jubilee Singers, have all been expended on the grounds and building; the ordinary expenditures, above receipts from students, having been met from the Treasury of the American Missionary Association, of New York City, under whose auspices all the movements of the University have been conducted.

The Association is, in its origin and history, identified with the efforts of American and British Christians for the overthrow of slavery and the evangelization of Africa. When the war opened the way for direct labors among the ex-slaves in America, it sent a large force of missionary teachers, who gathered Christian schools and formed churches in nearly every Southern state. More than forty thousand pupils were at one time taught in its schools.

It became manifest very soon that the progress of the people warranted more permanent methods. The people themselves were to become helpers in their own elevation. The rapid progress of the colored pupils demanded higher grades of schools in which they might be prepared as preachers, teachers, and leaders. Hence the opening of normal schools and colleges and the planting of churches. This policy has been pursued with most cheering results, as is witnessed by the growth of these institutions, the approbation of the people of the South, and the large number of colored teachers—male and female—which these schools have sent forth, together with the thousands of pupils they are now teaching.

The statistical tables published by the Association show that it has under its care in the South fifty-three churches, seven chartered institutions, some of them with permanent buildings, of which Fisk University (as shown in the plate) is a favorable specimen, seventeen normal and thirteen common schools. The church members number 3,227; the pupils in its schools 10,000; and those taught by its former students are estimated at 64,000.

The growth of this work is somewhat indicated by the increase of the Association's expenditure, from $16,517, the amount appropriated for 1862, to $273,088, which was paid out for Freedmen during 1873; and also by the fact that since the war of the rebellion began, it has collected and disbursed for the establishment and maintenance of its missions more than $2,736,280, or upwards of £500,000. The good already accomplished by such an institution as Fisk University cannot be stated or estimated; its student teachers for the year 1874, numbered 110. They taught an aggregate of 10,000 pupils, and earned $20,000.

To establish permanently a University for the colored people of the South, to educate the teachers of their schools and the pastors of their churches, and thus to lift up the race in this country and to turn a tide of Christian civilization to the shores and into the heart of Africa, is the object of the Jubilee Singers, the purpose of Fisk University, and the grand aim of the American Missionary Association.

E. M. C.

# CONTENTS.

### CHAPTER I.

Reorganization at Nashville—Preparations for two companies—Consolidation—Invitation to Philadelphia—No place for us in the Inns—Reception at Washington—Negroes refused reserved seats at Baltimore—Invitation to Princeton—Whites and Blacks separated in Church—Invitation to give Farewell Concert at Boston—Letter from the Governor of Tennessee—Prejudice shown by Steam Boat Companies—Farewell to America. . . . . . 1

### CHAPTER II.

English interest in Africa one reason for the success of the Jubilee Singers . . . . . . . . . 17

### CHAPTER III.

Arrive at Liverpool—Rev. James Powell—Introduction to Dr. Allon—Visit to the Earl of Shaftesbury—He arranges for Private Concert—Report of first meeting held in London—Invitation to the Duke of Argyll's—Commanded to appear and sing in the presence of Her Majesty the Queen . . . . . . 26

### CHAPTER IV.

Methods of work considered—Meeting in Union Chapel—Dinner and conversazione of the Congregational Union—Annual meeting of Freedmen's Missions Aid Society—Singers at Newman Hall's Sunday Service—Concerts at Surrey Chapel, St. James's Hall, and Hanover Square Rooms—Soirée of the National Temperance League—Opinions of the Press—Crystal Palace—Effect of Singing in Central Transept—Chorus by Five Thousand Children . . . . 42

### CHAPTER V.

London hospitalities—Mr. Samuel Gurney, of the Society of Friends—Visit to Botanical Gardens—Mr. George McDonald—Singing at a feast for the poor—Invitation to sing before the Prince and Princess

CONTENTS. xiii

PAGE

of Wales—Breakfast with the Right Hon. W. E. Gladstone—Letter by the Rev. Newman Hall—Singing on Sunday at Mr. Spurgeon's Metropolitan Tabernacle—Tea with Mr. Spurgeon—Concert at the Tabernacle—Departure for Scotland - - • • - 63

## CHAPTER VI.

Journey to Hull—Wilberforce Monument—Private Concert arranged by the Rev. W. C. Preston—Sunday Services—Open-air Service for the poor—Visit to training ship for boys—Successful Concert—Welcome to Scarborough by the Rev. R. Balgarnie—Private Concert —Great open-air Sunday School gathering—Preparations at Newcastle—Rev. H. T. Robjohns—Enthusiastic reception—Moody and Sankey at Sunderland—Importance of Patronage—Co-operation of Messrs. Common and Campbell—Crowded house • • • 90

## CHAPTER VII.

Visit to Castle-Wemyss—Welcome by Mr. and Mrs. John Burns—Singing at Garden Party—Address by Lord Shaftesbury—Reports of the Press—Service of Song at Gourock—Rev. David McRae—Concert at Greenock—Crowded house—Ex-Provost Morton's treat to working boys—Bailie Campbell—Bill of lading for cargo of slaves—Meeting at Hellenburgh - • • • - 103

## CHAPTER VIII.

Work done in Ireland—Opinions of the Irish Press—Irish interest in the Freedmen—Giant's Causeway—Londonderry—Historic associations—Work in Scotland—Welcome to Glasgow by the Lord Provost, Magistrates, and Town Council—Crowded house—Address by the Lord Provost—Visits to Perth, Dundee, and Aberdeen—Private Concert to distinguished persons—Welcome to Edinburgh by the City Government—Dinner with the Lord Provost—Letter from Dr. Hanna to Thomas Nelson—Sir Peter Coats—Presents of Paisley Shawls—Paisley Concerts—The Land of Burns—Dinner at Auchendrane—Critique by Mr. Colin Brown • - - 119

## CHAPTER IX.

Revival work—Moody and Sankey—Religious convention at Newcastle—Report by the Rev. H. T. Robjohns—Revival meetings in Edinburgh—Continued interest of the Jubilee Singers in revival work - • • • • • • • - 145

## CHAPTER X.

Darlington—Donations for Rooms—Singers at York—Alderman Leeman, M.P.—Private Concert at Bradford—Sir Titus Salt—Financial success at Leeds—Mr. John Crossley, M.P., of Halifax, promises carpeting—Second visit to Hull—Portrait of Wilberforce—Mr. John Bright—Mr. J. P. Barlow, of Bolton—Donation for rooms—Welcome to Manchester—Plan of work—Richard Johnson—Great financial success—Sickness—Concerts at Liverpool—Rev. Hugh Stowell Brown—Concerts at Sheffield and elsewhere—Death of Mrs. White—Welcome to Cambridge—President of the Midland Railway—School Board Agitations—Missionary Meeting - - - 159

## CHAPTER XI.

Effects of the Campaign on the Singers—Work done in Wales—Mr. Samuel Budgett of Bristol—Donations for rooms—George Müller—Plans for visiting Orphanage—Visit to Bath—Welcome back to London by Mr. Spurgeon—Presentation of books at the Concert in the Metropolitan Tabernacle—Work at Brighton and Southampton—Closing of the Campaign at Exeter Hall, London—The Earl of Shaftesbury—Address by the Rev. Henry Allon, D.D.—Address and presentation by Mr. Ransome—Reply by Mr. Holmes, of the Jubilee Singers—Closing address by Lord Shaftesbury—Return of the Singers to Nashville - - - - - - - 182

## JUBILEE SONGS.

PREFACE - - - - - - - - - 205
SONGS - - - - - - - - - 207
INDEX - - - - - - - - - 287

# THE SINGING CAMPAIGN

## FOR TEN THOUSAND POUNDS.

---

### CHAPTER I.

#### FAREWELL TO AMERICA.

FROM my earliest manhood I entertained the idea that if a person would accomplish a successful life, it would be fortunate for him to possess three things: the first was a renewed heart, the second, a liberal education, and the third, wealth. I argued that with these attainments he would become philanthropic, and gain a useful position among men; moreover, I believed that the education furnished by schools would be enlarged and made more valuable by travel. When, therefore, the Jubilee Singers' Campaign for £10,000 in Great Britain was ended, I hailed with joy the advent of my friend the doctor, who joined me in London, for a journey to the orient. I had not seen him since the story of the campaign for

$20,000 was published, and was happy to hear of the interest he had taken in its sale.

"The fact is," said the doctor one day, as we were gazing at a polished shaft in memory of Captain Speke, Victoria N'yanza, and the Nile, "I stimulated you to write that book, and believe that it has been of service to the American Missionary Association in its efforts on behalf of the African race: would not a second volume, narrating the experiences of the singers in the United Kingdom, encourage American Christians to continue their labours for the coloured man, and help him to become as much an object of respect as he has been of prejudice and hatred? I am a master of stenography," he went on to say, "and if you will narrate the history of your movements since we last were together, I will take notes and we can at our leisure prepare them for the press."

As by a comity of intercourse there is continuity of fellowship, I assented, provided that he would record his own observations during my recital; to this, after a modest apology, he accorded a pleasurable acquiescence. I hoped, therefore, for many valuable suggestions from his ripe reflections on missionary work, and in this I was not disappointed. Among his peculiarities was one respecting lofty eminences, either on mountains, hills, or towers. He argued that sharp elevated points of land, or artificial structures, broke the atmosphere and purified it; the winds, he said, that travel over mountain peaks, being lifted above the low grounds, were free from miasma, and developed the best type of character. He maintained also that our Creator had bestowed especial honour on hills and mountains. When He was about to give the law to Moses, he said, He did not visit him upon a plain, but on Mount Sinai; and when he sent His Son to exemplify the Law, and fulfil it, "seeing the multitude, He went up into a mountain, and taught them." Mount Horeb, Mount Zion, the Mount of Olives, Mount Calvary,—indeed, all the sacred hills in scripture story—were species of apostles, with their boon of wealth and influence, to his reverential mind. Following this impulse, we usually sought an elevated spot for our extended conversations, and when on a visit with him to the Crystal Palace, he asked me to ascend one of its towers, for a survey of London, and for rest; while I should relate to him the incidents of the Jubilee Singers' farewell to America.

"The Jubilee Singers," I said, "were reorganized at Nashville, after the completion of their first campaign, and the company enlarged to fifteen, for the purpose of accommodating smaller places with a quartette now and then, where it would not pay to send the whole company. Indeed, it was our purpose to monopolize the Jubilee Singers' business, arguing that, if Prof. White would use his superior skill and taste in teaching companies of our students in the south how to sing their old slave songs in the best possible manner, the American Missionary Association could supply the demand for the singers throughout the country, and, by such agencies, do much towards building up her many institutions, for the Christian education of the Freedmen. It was with this purpose in mind that two companies were trained during the summer months of 1872, and put into the field in the autumn of the same year. We had not, however, a sufficient organized working force for so extensive a business as two companies required, and the attempt to carry on this work without, only overcame and discouraged us. Accordingly, by the first of January, it was decided to unite our two companies and form a class with eleven of the best singers, and return the others to their homes; it was also decided about this time to inquire earnestly of one and another, in whose prudence and wisdom we could confide, concerning the expediency of making a venture in Great Britain, for the completion of the amount needful for Jubilee Hall, of the Fisk University, Nashville, Tennessee. The fact that we purposed to embark upon such a mission spurred on our friends in America to aid us. There is so much appreciation of heroism, that men lavish laudations on those who purpose it, and the benedictions bestowed upon the commencement of an enterprise are often as grateful as those bestowed upon the victors returning with the spoils. We took every opportunity, therefore, of informing the public that the Jubilee Singers would give grand farewell concerts in different towns before leaving for Europe. Several of these were significant, as to the usefulness of our mission, in overcoming prejudice; and especially those given in Philadelphia. Early in January I had been reflecting seriously upon projecting a series of concerts in that city, when I found myself one night suddenly awakened from a deep sleep with this thought in my mind, 'Visit George H. Stuart and others: their interest in the Freedmen may prompt them to co-operate in preparing the way for the Jubilee Singers to visit Philadelphia, and give a series of concerts for the benefit of Fisk University." The idea seemed practicable, so, after securing letters of introduction, I called upon Mr. Stuart the next day at his office and submitted the inquiry. He kindly invited me to spend the evening at his house, and after canvassing the subject, suggested that I should draw up a petition, and submit it to Horatio Gates Jones, Esq., inviting the Jubilee Singer troupe to Philadelphia, and that he would accompany me to his office the following day. This was accordingly done, and through the agency of Messrs. Stuart and Jones the subjoined invitation was signed and published as an item in the Philadelphia and New York papers:—

"'*Philadelphia, Jan. 8th*, 1873.

"'Gen. Clinton B. Fisk, President of Trustees of Fisk University, Nashville, Tennessee.

' 'Dear Sir,

"'We have learned with pleasure of the remarkable success of the Jubilee Singers of Fisk University. Their endeavour to earn $70,000 for the aid of the University meets our warmest approval.

"'The renown of their achievements at New York, Brooklyn, the World's Peace Jubilee at Boston, and other places, where they have attracted vast throngs of people to listen to the peculiar songs they have brought out of bondage, awakens in us great enthusiasm in their behalf. The fact that within less than a year they have earned more than a third of the amount they are seeking, assures us their efforts will be crowned with success. Will you not oblige us by visiting our city at an early day, in company with the singers, that our citizens may enjoy a series of their concerts?

"'We remain very respectfully yours,

"'George H. Stuart.       A. Whilldin.
    Jay Cooke.              John Wanamaker.
    Lemuel Coffin.          Richard Newton.
    Edward Hawes.           James Pollock.
    Horatio Gates Jones.    M. Simpson.'

"The influence of this petition was magical. At that time Jay Cooke was the foremost banker in America, Bishop Simpson was a masterly power in the Methodist Church, Richard Newton, D.D., stood without a rival as the author of a large number of sermons, and books for children, and·was rector of one of the most influential Episcopal Churches in the country. Indeed, each of the signatures indicated a representative man, and many of them had a national reputation.

"The fact that the Jubilee Singers were to be in a measure the guests of such men was enough to ensure a grand reception. The Academy of Music in Philadelphia is the most elegant and commodious of any in the country. Notwithstanding that it had been refused to a U.S. senator, some months before, because of his colour, the influence of the gentlemen inviting the singers was sufficient to secure it; and the fact that the coloured band were the first representatives of the African race ever permitted to appear on its platform, made the advent of the concert an epoch in the history of the city. The Hon. George H. Stuart entered into the business of this series of concerts with all the enthusiasm of his benevolent nature. Jay Cooke occupied a prominent place in one of the boxes, and Mr. Horatio Gates Jones was as untiring in every particular as though the success of the whole enterprise rested upon him.

"The vast building was thronged from floor to ceiling, and afforded a most magnificent spectacle.

"My business associate, Mr. Isaac W. Hutchins, had spent two days and a half in attempting to secure accommodation for the students in some hotel, but had failed altogether, and finally was compelled to lodge them in a coloured boarding-house; so, in thanking the audience for their generous patronage, I improved the occasion, by calling their attention to the prejudice against colour that was yet to be overcome. I told them it happened to us as in days gone by to One whom angels welcomed, that there was no room for us in the inn; that Mr. Hutchins found no hotel proprietor brave enough to risk the odium he might incur if he lodged negroes. The audience was one of the grandest of the season in every way, and was at a high pitch of enthusiasm when this statement was made; and their murmurs of disapproval were very significant. Many moments had not transpired when a man of gentlemanly appearance came to me, and said that I was mistaken; that he was the proprietor of one of the largest hotels in the city, and had not declined to receive the singers. I explained that he was away when Mr. Hutchins called, and if my statement was unjust I would correct the error. Before the close of the concert, therefore, I made it known that the Continental Hotel, which scarcely had a superior in the world, would entertain the coloured students; this announcement was received with great approbation, while a report of the circumstance found its way into the papers, and served to create a healthy opinion among the hotel-keepers. Subsequently the singers took up their quarters at the Continental, and were treated with much attention both by proprietor and guests. The series of concerts inaugurated by these methods were the most successful of any ever given by us in America. From Philadelphia we proceeded to Washington, where we received an ovation in the Association Hall that nearly resulted in a riot, so great was the throng of people. On our return, we stopped at Baltimore, memorable for its riot in the early part of the rebellion.

"Mr. Hutchins had secured the use of the Masonic Hall, a beautiful building in the central part of the city, and through the agency of my friend, the Rev. Cyrus Osborne, had arranged for the sale of tickets at a first-class music warehouse. The ticket-seller took the liberty of assuring the whites that no negroes would be admitted to the body of the hall, and declined to sell reserved seat tickets on the floor to the coloured people. On our arrival, learning these facts, as much to our dissatisfaction as to the negroes, and ascertaining that neither the proprietors of the hall, Mr. Hutchins, nor Mr. Osborne had provided for, or assented to, any such arrangement, I went to the hall-door, relieved the ticket-seller, and, stationing myself in the box, proclaimed that any person wishing a seat in any part of the house could have it by paying the advertised price, and further, that if the ushers and doorkeepers demurred, they would be discharged and others employed. A few coloured men bought reserved seat tickets, and occupied places in the body of the house without giving, so far as I know, the slightest offence. Indeed, the applause of the audience was so frequent and hilarious throughout the evening that it seemed as though we never would have done with the programme. The proceeds of the concert were remarkable, considering the pro-slavery history of Baltimore.

"About this time I received a letter signed by Pres. McCosh and the faculty of Princeton College, asking the singers to visit Princeton, and give a service of song in one of their churches. As the state of New Jersey had been a scene of many trials to Mr. White on account of prejudice against the colour of his band, we were glad to have such complimentary notice; and I availed myself of the opportunity to fix a date for accepting the invitation. It was not possible for me to be present on the occasion, but I afterwards learned that Prof. White found, on his arrival with the students, a portion of the church reserved for the coloured people; while all authorities absolutely refused them admittance elsewhere. Mr. White and the singers were naturally very indignant, and would gladly have given up the concert, had it not been too late. They proceeded, therefore, with a determination to utter a protest. Prof. White felt that, after giving concerts for two seasons without being subjected to such an indignity, even in a public hall, it was a grievance not to be passed over in silence when asked to make an invidious distinction in a church of Christ against the very class of people who gave the performance, and especially when this demand was countenanced by the distinguished educators of a Christian College, who might be presumed to hate all manner of prejudice with a holy hatred. So at an interval during the concert he expressed his sentiments without reserve. The singers were kindly treated by President McCosh, and I have no reason to suppose that he approved of the injustice shown; indeed, every one seemed captivated with the music, and charitable towards the students; while Mr. White, for the time, was obliged to bear a censure that shall some day be glorified to a crown, when the night of prejudice has passed away.

"About this time farewell concerts were given in Mr. Beecher's church, Brooklyn; in New York City; Newark, N. J.; Boston; Providence, and elsewhere. Prior to the one at Boston, I received the following letter, which was presented to me through the kindness of Mr. Briggs, who had acted in concert with Messrs. Curtis, Bacup, and B. W. Williams, chief of the American Literary Bureau, in providing for the éclat of the last appearance of the singers in New England:—

"'*Boston, Feb. 26th,* 1873.

"'Rev. G. D. Pike.

"'Dear Sir,—

"'Understanding that the Jubilee Singers from Fisk University, whose concerts afforded us so much pleasure last season, are about to visit Europe in the endeavour to add to the fund already secured by their efforts in aid of the University, and being desirous to testify to our hearty sympathy with the cause in which they are engaged, we would respectfully request that, in addition to the two concerts already advertised to be given in this city, they give a grand farewell Concert in the Music Hall, on the evening of March 26th. With our best wishes for their future success, we remain,

" 'Very respectfully yours,

" 'Thomas Russell.     John Bacup.
 Alex. H. Rice.     Edward E. Hale.
 George B. Loring.    Wendell Phillips.
 William Claflin.     Phillips Brooks.
 Edward N. Kirk.     Wm. Loyd Garrison.

" 'And many others.'

"This invitation, with the reply signed by Prof. White and myself, was published in the papers. The price of reserved seats was fixed at one dollar, and the movement assumed a very popular aspect. Although the evening for the service was rainy, the house was well filled. Brief addresses were made, and farewell benedictions given by the Mayor, and other distinguished persons who occupied the platform. The financial result exceeded that of any previous concert given by us in Boston; and I think it is not too much to say, that no young people ever bid farewell to their country laden with so many attentions and good wishes as these children of recent bondage, who had been so admirably illustrating the elastic energy of the Black man, when afforded an equal opportunity with others in the race of life. If the good wishes of the American people could have purchased for the singers success in Great Britain, their triumph would have been assured.

"Already I had provided myself with letters of recommendation from the Governors of five of the New England States; and Prof. White had received one from the Governor of Tennessee. I also had letters from Henry Ward Beecher, George H. Stuart, George McDonald, Mark Twain, General John Eaton, U. S. Commissioner of Education at Washington, General C. B. Fisk, and many others. I will only give in this place two of these letters; the first is the one sent to Mr. White by the Governor of Tennessee, as indicating official sentiment in a State where, only a short time previous, the people were hostile to the elevation of the negro; the other, that of Mark Twain.

'"*Executive Office, State of Tennessee,*
'"*March 25th*, 1873.
"'To whom it may concern.

"'The Jubilee Singers, under charge of Prof. Geo. L. White, purpose sailing for Europe in a few days, in the interest of Jubilee Hall, of Fisk University, in contemplation of being erected at Nashville, Tennessee. . . . I need not say that the work in which they are engaged commends itself to the hearty approval of every philanthropist and friend of education and religion, and I bespeak for them the largest sympathy, patronage, and encouragement. They are pioneers in a great movement by the coloured people to educate themselves, and the experiment is looked to with interest. This class of our population needs to be educated, and that subject is beginning to receive the attention its importance demands. The embarrassments in the South, growing out of the great loss of property by the late war, are rapidly disappearing; but we are yet poor, and I sincerely hope that the efforts of this party may be fully rewarded by their contemplated visit to Europe.

"'JNO. C. BROWN,
"'Governor of Tennessee.'

*Hartford, March* 10.

To TOM HOOD, Esq., and MESSRS. GEORGE ROUTLEDGE & SONS, London:

Gentlemen:

The Jubilee Singers are to appear in London, and I am requested to say in their behalf what I know about them—and I most cheerfully do it.

I heard them sing once, and I would walk seven miles to hear them sing again. You will recognize that this is strong language for me to use, when you remember that I never was fond of pedestrianism, and got tired of walking, that Sunday afternoon, in twenty minutes, after making up my mind to see for myself and at my own leisure how much ground his grace the Duke of Bedford's property covered.

I think these gentlemen and ladies make eloquent music—and what is as much to the point, they reproduce the true melody of the plantations, and are the only persons I ever heard accomplish this on the public platform. The so-called "negro minstrels" simply mis-represent the thing; I do not think they ever saw a plantation or ever heard a slave sing.

I was reared in the South, and my father owned slaves, and I do not know when anything has so moved me as did the plaintive melodies of the Jubilee Singers. It was the first time for twenty-five or thirty years that I had heard such songs, or heard them sung in the genuine old way—and it is a way, I think, that white people cannot imitate—and never can, for that matter, for one must have been a slave himself in order to feel what that life was and so convey the pathos of it in the music. Do not fail to hear the Jubilee Singers. I am very well satisfied that you will not regret it.    Yours faithfully,

SAML. L. CLEMENS.
MARK TWAIN.


"But," interrupted the doctor, "how about the departure of the singers?"

"Previously to my sailing," I said, "I had spent two days at New York endeavouring to secure a good passage for them. I did not inquire at all the first-class steamship companies, but, so far as I did inquire, I got refusals, as the agents feared the passengers would not like to have negroes to accompany them in the cabins. Sick at heart, I went on to Boston, where I hoped a better atmosphere might prevail. There I found no difficulty in getting them booked by the Cunard Steamer, 'Batavia,' upon which boat they were treated with much consideration by the officers and passengers, during the entire voyage."

## CHAPTER II.

ENGLISH INTEREST IN AFRICA—A REASON FOR THE
SUCCESS OF THE JUBILEE SINGERS.

THE doctor and I found, on making inquiries about the best routes to the continent and the East, that much we had anticipated respecting the remoteness of foreign countries was dispelled. We could go to Brussels in ten hours, to Paris in ten hours, to Geneva in twenty-eight, to Italy in thirty-six, to Rome in two days, to Egypt in six days, and to the Holy Land with but seven days' travelling. This information really took from us a good deal of enthusiasm, and so unsettled our minds that it would not have added materially to our bewilderment if we had been told, as well, that we might go back in a week not only to the old places but to the old times, and see Joseph selling grain in Egypt, or, indeed, mother Eve dressing her hair on the banks of the Euphrates. We were disappointed in learning that we need take nothing for our journey, for we could buy anything we might wish in any of the continental or oriental cities. A rubber suit might be convenient if there were rains in Palestine. No pistol, or dirk, no cooking apparatus, or supply of condiments, nothing but bank of England notes in abundance, with a "Murray or two"; so the half-day before our departure for Paris was on our hands, and the doctor suggested that we should ascend to the golden gallery of St. Paul's, where, from an elevation of three hundred and fifty feet, we could take a farewell survey of London, from a site sacred for worship for more than a thousand years, and renowned for the finest Protestant Cathedral in the world. On this historic spot the doctor proposed that we should spend an hour, while I answered a question he had often asked, which was, "What English interest in Africa had to do with the remarkable success of the Jubilee Singers in England?"

"That interest," I said, "was a special Providence in our favour. The English are very fond of explorations and discoveries. Living on a narrow island, they stretch their aims and arms over the broad earth any part of the globe not entirely discovered or explored is to them a golden opportunity to add to the extent of their domains and the glory of their achievements. Africa has been a land of unknown possibilities to them; they have believed 'its sunny fountains rolled down their golden sands.' What wealth is concealed in her fastnesses? What paradise is enclosed in her vast interior, guarded by the lion, the elephant, the rhinoceros, and the hippopotamus, with swamps and miasma as their bulwarks of defence? What mountains, under an equatorial sun, tower heavenward to altitudes where rests the eternal snow? What lakes contain the springs from which issue forth the mighty Nile, the Niger, and the Zambezi? What people dwell in haunts wrapped in sacred mystery? What form of beast resembling man lurks to destroy, defying ordinary methods of defence, and bold to push his conquest till his enemies perish at his feet? What birds, what flowers, what fruits, what spices, what woods, what metals? Indeed, what may there not be in realms unknown, or lakes or mountains unexplored? These questions come home to British Islanders. They stimulate to great enterprise.

"Eighty years ago Mungo Park landed on the banks then returned to England, and astonished the nation then returned to England, and electrified the nation with his stories of African regions. Such interest was awakened that henceforth the explorations of Africa were conducted by Government, and immense sums of money were expended.

"Five thousand pounds were placed at Park's disposal, and with forty white soldiers he pursued his discoveries. Clapperton and the Lander brothers went forth, and in their turn kept alive the interest awakened by Mungo Park, until the questions about the Niger were settled.

"Bruce, a native of Scotland, wandered in Africa and elsewhere for years, and gave to the world the story of his travels, which read like a romance, and excited the wonder of the young and the suspicions of the old, till every paper made common cause in ridiculing him as an unworthy authority respecting African regions; but nevertheless he did much to sustain an interest in African explorations; indeed, before his death, we are told that 'African travel became a mania that affected all enterprising minds.' First, public curiosity seemed interested in the Niger and the west coast; but later on, great enthusiasm was manifested in ascertaining the source of the Nile. Expeditions were sent out, and money expended without stint, till the tales of the travellers would fill a library. The numerous books on Africa were sure to be purchased with great avidity, and to reward the author with rich returns: I have heard it said that the profits realized by Dr. Livingstone on one of his publications amounted to ten thousand pounds. These things have been transpiring for seventy-five years.

"Another influence had been at work as well. The English people are liberty-loving, and earnest in charitable and humane enterprises. No nation in the world has such absorbing interest in relieving the unfortunate and alleviating the suffering of mankind; her asylums, her hospitals, and other benevolent institutions are thick as the stars, and as brilliant in her history. Where suffering is the greatest, there her eye turns with lightning rapidity, and her heart goes forth with great gushes of sympathy and affection. The horrors of slavery, therefore, were sure to arrest her most earnest attention: her great statesmen gave to it their ripest reflections, her distinguished philanthropists achieved their highest fame when battling for its overthrow in every land. The name of Wilberforce is held as sacred in consequence of his labours for emancipation as the names of great reformers who were true to the faith, and suffered as martyrs for the overthrow of Roman Catholicism. Even the John Brown song was the famous music of the British soldiers in the Ashantee war of 1873 on the west coast of Africa.

"Dr. Livingstone, in his travels through the southern portions of Africa, taught the natives to believe that, when they were sure a traveller was an Englishman, they might know he detested slavery. But still further it must be added that, during the past fifteen years, the efforts of Burton, who made his journey across Africa; of Speke and Grant, who discovered Victoria N'yanza; and of Sir Samuel Baker and his wife, who journeyed to the Albert N'yanza; and of Dr. Livingstone, Dr. Moffat, H. M. Stanley, and others, have flooded the country with a fresh enthusiasm by their untiring efforts. The present generation has been supplied with information and conjecture sufficient for a literature in itself.

"A new revelation respecting the lake system of

Central Africa has electrified the world. During all these years the church had not been asleep; the pious people had taken as much interest in the salvation of the souls of the poor pagan as the explorer had in his wonderful country. The Church Missionary Society had established a large number of schools and missions, and now expends about $95,000 per year in Africa. Last year there were under training more than fifteen thousand children in school as the result of their labours. The London Missionary Society since 1816 has been extending its missions on the west coast and in other places, and by its wide operations has done a great work, and at present is expending $36,000 per annum. The Wesleyan Missionary Society is in advance of every other, and expends now $125,000 yearly, and sustains seventeen thousand children in its schools in Africa. The Baptist Mission in 1873 expended $13,000 for African labours. Many other missions, some of which are of a more private character, expend in the aggregate $31,000 annually. When we sum up the different amounts, we find the English give in money $300,000 per year for the conversion of the Africans, besides the sons and daughters needful to carry on the work. The educational influence of so much given and received is very great. At the anniversary meetings, which are crowded with throngs of people from all over the land, the missionaries on visits from Africa to their fatherland are welcomed with great enthusiasm, and their narratives of African life listened to with the deepest interest by the appreciative audience. As the beating of the heart sends the blood merrily to the remotest part of the body, so the pulsations of these great anniversary meetings of foreign missions send out intelligence, enthusiasm, and life, to the ends of the United Kingdom. The grandest convocation in the world is a great missionary meeting, and men who participate in it become inoculated with a new life, which never entirely dies out. Such influences as these I have mentioned had been preparing the way for a mission like that of the Jubilee Singers. When I arrived in London I found that Sir Bartle Frere had just returned from the east coast of Africa, where he had been, as an agent of the Government, to negociate for the suppression of the slave trade. Public meetings were held, and the enthusiasm manifested at his success of the most cheering character. He seemed to me to be the lion of London just at that time. The Rev. Charles New, a Wesleyan missionary, had returned from the east coast, at which place he had made explorations, penetrating to the interior as far as the snow mountains in the vicinity of the equator, and his labours were being made known and his name prominent as a speaker and writer. The Ashantee war was going on, and the daily papers, through their war correspondents, fed their readers with a course on Africa nearly every day, and even the theatres did not consider a play complete unless somewhere they introduced the king of the Ashantees."

"I have noticed," said the doctor, "some of these things already. Did you not observe Madame Tussaud advertising her wax-works by flaming notices announcing that she has portrait models of Livingstone and H. M. Stanley?"

"To be sure," I said; "and almost as much honour has been bestowed upon Sir Garnet Wolseley since his return from his African war as though he were another Moses, come up from Egypt."

"And," continued the doctor, "doubtless the fact that the British govern a portion of Southern and Western Africa adds to their interest very considerably."

"Yes," I said; "and as they need Egypt for a half-way house to India, and as the passage-way for their vessels is through the Suez Canal, it is certain the land of pyramids, diamonds, pearls, and gold, has not a finished history in respect to its Government."

"Just so," said the doctor. "And when I attended the funeral of Dr. Livingstone, and saw his bones deposited in Westminster Abbey, Nonconformist though he was, when I saw England in mourning for that great man, whose name was too sacred to be supplemented by any title it was in her power to bestow, I took heart in praying for Africa."

"I, too," I said, "have had many occasions of mentioning one name and another, as I have appeared before thousands of the people of this country; and whenever I have mentioned the name of Livingstone I have found a response that told me that he and his labours were loved as though his enterprise was the affair of every large town in the three kingdoms."

"This field was indeed made white for your harvest," said the doctor; "my question is abundantly answered. Let us go down from these heights and take our departure for Paris."

## CHAPTER III.

### WELCOME OF THE SINGERS TO LONDON.

WHILE the doctor and I were on our way to Paris, we were impressed with the difference in the general appearance of France from England and the more settled portions of America.

"I think," said the doctor, "that Catholicism does not promote the general good appearance of the rural districts. I understand that out of about thirty-six millions of inhabitants in France, nearly thirty-five millions are Catholics."

"Education," I said, "is not general or liberal in Catholic communities, and so the mass of the people are not elevated; furthermore, charitable institutions unconnected with the Church or State are almost unknown. The inhabitants of a country must have their better qualities of mind developed by normal and free acts of benevolence in order to give a moral beauty to their institutions. Catholicism levies taxes: Protestantism depends upon the application of those loving principles which elevate the whole moral nature, when money or labour is needful for the amelioration of mankind—so the average Protestant betters himself while bettering others—which is not true of the average Catholic."

With such reflections as these we journeyed on to Paris. I shall never forget the impression made upon my mind by this wonderful city; I thought it the theatre of the world. Its beauty, its gaiety, its intoxicating splendours hardly seemed compatible with real life; they filled my ideal of Dreamland.

The doctor and I roamed about for days through gardens and groves, with walks and shades, "fit haunts of God," till one day we climbed to the summit of the Triumphal Arch, to review some of the achievements of the *Third Napoleon*.

"We now live," said the doctor, "in an age of peace; though wars do still occur, yet they are not considered a desirable occupation for mankind. He who brings to light some great invention, he who introduces some valuable improvement that adds largely to our comfort, is a greater benefactor than one who stains his hands with blood. And when I see these spacious avenues, adorned with groves and flowers, and resonant with the pattering play of crystal fountains, and with the songs of birds, that allure the traveller on beneath the arching boughs and mellow shade; when I look over this broad area of city, and behold on every hand monuments that mark the peaceful reign of the last Napoleon, I believe that as the age of peace rolls on, the people of France will awaken to admire the vast improvements which he instituted more lovingly than ever they did his uncle's deeds of war."

"As the Spirit of Christ becomes more prevalent," I said, "the spirit of war must either cease altogether or abide in dishonour among the more ignorant."

By this time the doctor had his note-book on his knees, and having secured a couple of chairs from the vendor of opera-glasses and photographs, he asked, that I should tell him about the welcome of the Jubilee Singers to England, and so I went on to say,—

"I arrived at Liverpool, accompanied by the Rev. James Powell, on the 8th of April, and proceeded the next day to London. Mr. Powell was a native of Wales, and, knowing something of English life, kindly came with me for the purpose of rendering assistance in securing a favourable introduction for the singers in London. On the day of our arrival we called at Messrs. Hodder and Stoughton's, publishers, in Paternoster Row, and acquainted Mr. Hodder with the object of our visit; without hesitation he promised us his most earnest support, and I believe that through him we secured the prayers and sympathy of many active workers in the Young Men's Christian Association—of which he is an influential member. I mention this because you must bear in mind that all our successful work was begun with prayer, and that we relied upon its power to aid us in surmounting all obstacles.

"My most important letters of introduction were addressed to the Rev. Henry Allon, D.D., pastor of Union Chapel, London. They were from the Revs. Henry Ward Beecher, George McDonald, and Henry M. Dexter, D.D. I posted them to Dr. Allon and requested an interview, which was accorded me at an early date; he entered most heartily into the consideration of the question, "How to do it," and freely offered us the use of his chapel for our first meeting. The committee of the Young Men's Christian Association also offered their building and assistance in bringing the singers before the public; but the more I understood the methods of the English, the more I came to appreciate the vast importance of securing the patronage of the pious nobility in furthering a benevolent enterprise. The Freedmen's Mission Aid Society had, at the time of its organization, enlisted the sympathies of the Right Hon. Earl of Shaftesbury, and he had accepted its presidency; no man in the country was better known, and all the friends of our enterprise appreciated the importance of obtaining the influence of his name at the outset. The Rev. Dr. Healy, the corresponding secretary of the society, in company with the Rev. Mr. Jones, of the Turkish Mission Aid Society, volunteered to call with me upon his lordship, and consult respecting what ought first to be done. Mr. Hodder had procured for us a letter of introduction from Mr. Shipton, secretary of the Young Men's Christian Association, commending in the kindest way the mission of the singers. Armed with this document and several others, Dr. Healy, Mr. Jones, and myself waited upon his lordship, and were informed that he was going out to a meeting and that we must call the next day; we left our documents, however.

"I am convinced, from such information as I have been able to gather, that the noble earl may be justly ranked as the foremost philanthropist in the world. He has passed the age of threescore and ten, and has been engaged for more than forty years in promoting great benevolent enterprises. His interest has been chiefly manifested in the amelioration of the condition of the poor. Nothing perhaps will better illustrate the quality of the man than the fact that when the position of Lord Lieutenant of Ireland was offered him, with an income of £20,000 per annum, equal to $100,000, he declined it on the ground that he wished to be free to secure the passage of a bill in the House of Lords, for the improvement of the condition of factory operatives. This act appears all the more admirable in the light of the fact that he is not wealthy for a nobleman. We found that he carried on a regular business of receiving calls during certain hours, from persons interested in all manner of benevolent projects. Visitors are shown into a reception room, and often must wait an hour for their turn in company with others seeking an interview.

"Dr. Healy and myself found upon a second visit that his lordship had read Mr. Shipton's letter, and was somewhat apprised of our mission. I shall never forget the readiness with which he entered into our project; when Dr. Healy or myself, I do not remember which, told him of our purpose, and with some anxiety asked if he would consent to take the chair at the first appearance of the Jubilee Singers, he immediately answered, "I should be most happy to do so," and then suggested that a private concert be given, and persons invited to it in the name of the Freedmen's Mission Aid Society. Subsequently the following card was prepared:—

THE EARL OF SHAFTESBURY,

PRESIDENT,

WITH THE COUNCIL AND COMMITTEE OF THE FREEDMEN'S MISSION AID SOCIETY,

REQUEST THE FAVOUR OF

COMPANY AT A

PRIVATE CONCERT OF THE JUBILEE SINGERS

(OF FISK UNIVERSITY, NASHVILLE, TENNESSEE, U.S.A.),

AT WILLIS'S ROOMS,

ON TUESDAY NEXT, THE 6TH OF MAY.

TO COMMENCE AT THREE O'CLOCK PRECISELY.

24, GROSVENOR SQUARE, W.,
April 30th, 1873.

"On the envelope enclosing this card, at the left-hand corner near the bottom, the word Shaftesbury was lithographed, and this alone would call immediate and favourable attention to it.

"These were supplied to clergymen of different denominations, to editors, and to influential people likely to be interested in the movement. Lord Shaftesbury kindly sent many to his personal friends, and used his vast influence to make the service in every way successful. Mr. Powell and myself had secured favourable notices of the advent of the singers in many of the papers, both religious and secular, and indeed had occupied nearly a month in arousing an enthusiasm in behalf of the mission. We reasoned that if we could secure at our first meeting representatives of the different religious denominations, and a full supply of reporters, we should have the best possible agents at work for the enterprise in the churches, and in the columns of the press, and, moreover, we thought that, it being anniversary time, representatives from all parts of the kingdom would be visiting London, who might be influenced to aid us in the provinces. In none of these things were we disappointed. At this time we were indebted to the advice of Mr. George Dolby, who had achieved such wonderful success in company with Mr. Charles Dickens in America. Mr. Dolby's great experience in providing for public readings, and concerts of a high order, fitted him to counsel us respecting the observance of such proprieties as are acceptable to the intelligent people in England.

"When the day of the concert arrived, no stone had been left unturned that could add to a fitting preparation for the event. The large room was crowded to overflowing. Among the distinguished guests were the Duke and Duchess of Argyll, Lady Edith Ashley, the Honourable Lionel and Mrs. Ashley, Mr. McArthur M.P., Dr. Stephens, Q.C., and a large number of the leading divines of the country.

"The Earl of Shaftesbury made a few introductory remarks, after which the singers proceeded with their programme. I cannot do better in telling of the effect produced by their first appearance than quote from a report in one of the music periodicals of London. It says,—

"'They arranged themselves in front of the platform in a phalanx three deep. They stand with head erect and somewhat thrown back, and looking upwards, or with eyes nearly closed. It is evident the audience is nothing to them, they are going to make music and listen to one another. Their first song was, "Steal away to Jesus." It was sung slowly; the first chords came floating on our senses like gentle fairy music, and they were followed by the unison of phrase, "Steal away—to Jesus," delivered with exquisite precision of time and accent; then came the soft chords, and bold unison again, followed by the touching, throbbing cadence, "I hain't got long to stay here"; next follows the loud, lofty trumpet call in unison, " My Lord calls me, the trumpet sounds it in my soul; I hain't got long to stay here." But it seems as though the angels also were speaking to the sufferer, for we hear again those beautiful chords delivered with double pianissimo, whispering to the soul, "Steal away to Jesus."'

"Although all present might not endorse the high encomiums bestowed by this writer on the quality of the singing, yet I am sure he spoke for the whole when he said, 'Now blessings on these brave young students of the Fisk University.'

"During a brief recess in the concert, Dr. Allon read the following letter from Henry Ward Beecher, which was received with great applause:—

*Brooklyn, N.Y., U.S.A., March* 13*th,* 1873.

"'My Dear Mr. Allon,—

"'I wish to commend to your active sympathy the "Jubilee Singers," who will sail on the 11th April for Great Britain.

"'They are, by their singing, raising funds for the building of Fisk University, in Tennessee. Such a work was never attempted before, and it now seems certain that a University for the education of the coloured people of the South will be endowed by the songs of a band of young men and women who were almost all of them born in slavery, and several of whom have been repeatedly sold from master to master. You will hear from them the wild slave songs, some of which seem like the inarticulate wails of breaking hearts made dumb by slavery; you will hear the Revival Melodies, the plantation songs, in short, the inner life of slave hearts, expressed in music. It is hardly probable that ever again you will have a chance like this.

"'Their success has been wonderful. Already they have raised more than forty thousand dollars in America—all of which is put into buildings. Every brick thus is, as it were, a musical note. You may venture upon receiving this corps with the utmost confidence. The managers are men of good sense, integrity, and of devoted piety. We are not ashamed to send this band to our British brethren, and we are sure that their music will strike a chord which will vibrate long after their songs shall cease.

"'With great affection, etc.,

"'HENRY WARD BEECHER.'

"The singers acquitted themselves in the best possible manner, fully realizing how much depended upon their *début*, and, ambitious as ever young people were, to earn the good-will of all who heard them. They had carried their audience by storm before the programme was half-way over, and triumph was assured.

"At the close of the service showers of congratulations were received, while offers of co-operation were very abundant. I think it was Lord Shaftesbury who introduced me to the Duke of Argyll, who in turn presented me to the Duchess. During our conversation I was asked by them how they could further our object, and was invited to visit Argyll Lodge in Kensington together with the singers. Nothing could have been more acceptable to any of us, and before we parted it was arranged that our visit should take place the next day.

"The morning papers were lavish in their praise of the object and worthiness of the singers. The *Stand-*

*ard* said, 'It is the best entertainment of its kind ever brought out in London.' The *Times*, after quoting from Mr. Beecher's and Mr. McDonald's letters to Dr. Allon, in which the ability of the singers was highly eulogised, said, 'We cannot say that the expectations raised by these praises have been disappointed.' The *Daily News* said, 'The audience listened with the utmost sympathy and attention;' and the *Telegraph*, that 'The singers were manifestly destined to take a prominent position among the most remarkable attractions of the present season,' and that the private concert 'more than justified the strong recommendations with which the Jubilee Singers came accredited.' Indeed, a volume could be filled with what was sooner or later written in explanation and praise of the first appearance of the singers in England.

"We had, by this time, gotten a leverage, and it remained for us to make the best of it. No sooner was our anxiety relieved by the success of the private concert than we were called to a new experience. We knew nothing of the customs of the nobility. We had heard, however, of the liberality of the Duke of Argyll, whom we were about to visit, and read his able productions on antislavery questions. We hoped, therefore, as our cause was benevolent, we should be able to find kind consideration on the ground of our good purposes, especially if we avoided all affectation.

"I think we reached Argyll Lodge about four o'clock The ladies of the party, including Miss Gilbert and Mrs. White, were conducted to proper apartments and the gentlemen waited their return, when we were shown into a drawing-room, overlooking a large garden. Here we found a dozen or more people awaiting our arrival. The Duke, the Duchess, and one of their daughters welcomed us and spared no pains in entertaining us.

The singers were occupied, singing and conversing with one and another, while Prof. White and myself were answering questions. We were intensely anxious that the opening afforded us to the best-appreciated families of the kingdom might not be closed because of any inattention on our part. During these moments of friendly intercourse the countenance and conversation of a middle aged lady inspired me with confidence in her as an adviser. Placing myself under her direction as to what would be most acceptable to the Duke and Duchess, and befitting the occasion, I said I should be most grateful if she would advise me as to the proprieties of the interview, and indicate when it would be best for us to retire. With as much care and kindness as though she were the mother of us all, she put my mind at rest. What was my gratification to learn afterwards that she was one of the Queen's most intimate friends, 'and perhaps the most accomplished and respected woman in the kingdom.' I am sure I never met a person in any country who seemed to possess so many qualifications for making every one, from the smallest child to the Queen herself, happy and at home in her presence. During our conversation I manifested solicitude, fearing we should extend our interview beyond the rules of propriety; but she bade me 'be patient,' as the Queen was expected soon. What that announcement was to us no other person can ever appreciate; we had been told if we could but sing to Her Majesty our success would be assured, and that by all means we must make it our purpose to get an early audience with Her Majesty. But how could eleven coloured children, eight of whom were recently slaves, command her attention? How could I do it on behalf of a Missionary Society? Men with millions could not necessarily procure an interview. How could Prof. White do so? Men seeking money for a charity are not necessarily welcomed in kings' palaces! We learned, however, that the eldest son of the Duke of Argyll had married one of the Queen's daughters, and this would account for her coming. The Duke and Duchess well knew the prestige it would give the singers to appear before Her Majesty, and I have been told that, as she was coming to London that day, they had invited her to their residence for the very purpose of benefiting the Jubilee Singers. From Lady Augusta Stanley I understood it was possible the Queen might command the students to sing in her presence.

"On her arrival the silence of respect and of expectation fell upon all present, and the quickened tension of our nerves evinced our deep interest in the events just before us. By-and-by, one after another of the Queen's attendants came to positions where the singers could be seen and heard, a few songs were sung, and many questions asked, till at length the Duke entered and announced to Prof. White that the Queen would be pleased to see him with the singers in an adjoining room. Prof. White, the students, and myself followed His Grace into Her Majesty's presence, and stood before a ruler upon whose domain the sun never sets. I think her daughter Beatrice was standing near her. I thought the pictures I had seen of her failed to do her justice: the refinement in her manner was mellowed by the tender look that is only worn by a loving and generous parent. I instinctively thought that one could not fare ill if he committed himself to her kindness and mercy; and since that day I have never wondered at England's love for her Sovereign.

"By the request of the Duke, 'Steal away to Jesus' was sung, and followed by the chanting of 'The Lord's Prayer'; then, after a short pause, 'Go down, Moses,' a song that they had sung at the White House in Washington, before President Grant. But little conversation was carried on, and that took place between Her Majesty and the Duke, who told us she was much pleased, and thanked us for our kindness. As we retired the Queen graciously bowed, and we withdrew to the room where refreshments had been prepared.

"We endeavoured to assure the Duke and Duchess we were quite sensible of the service they had rendered. Both of them, however, are too great and good to encumber those benefited with a feeling of obligation.

"This act of theirs grows more and more beautiful as weeks and months roll by, and leads me to believe that the nobility born of the gospel, when allied to noble birth, becomes more potent for good.

"Before leaving Argyll Lodge we had accepted an invitation from Dean Stanley to visit the Deanery at Westminster Abbey. After returning the singers to Upper Norwood, Prof. White and myself spent the entire evening in laborious duties connected with the further prosecution of our campaign, now so auspiciously opened, but the toil seemed easy. I was obliged to spend an hour walking about (the rain was pouring down) trying to find lodgings for the night, so crowded are all the city hotels at this season of the year. Our hearts, however, were joyous and light. We had embarked on an untried career, upon a foreign shore; we had sped our way, borne on the bosom of ten thousand prayers, and resting on the arms of sympathy and of great love. The gates had been opened, and obstacles removed, with the same power by which the 'walls of Jericho fell down.' We were in a land of promise, the Queen had bidden us welcome, and it needed no pressing exhortation to inspire us to 'wait on the Lord, and to be of good courage.'"

## CHAPTER IV.

#### WORK DONE IN LONDON.

THE best route from Paris to Geneva passes Macon and Culoz, and the easiest train leaves Paris early in the evening. The doctor and I concluded to take this train, though we were thus obliged to miss a view of much which might have been seen on the way. Our disappointment when reaching the banks of the Rhone was considerable; it seemed absurd that so insignificant a river should be famous the world over. But the vine-clad hills on either side, extending for miles, gave evidence of an industry worthy of great praise. When an American reaches Geneva he is at once possessed with a home-feeling: there is liberty in the air, there is a democracy hundreds of years old, and he can but wonder if the American States did not borrow much from this land when she framed her government. Class distinctions are not very marked, and no offence is given by the servility of the poorer and no servility of the poorer classes is apparent.

The doctor and I went to Lausanne, passed Berne, and Interlacken, till we came to the beautiful lake

Thun, upon which we embarked in a little steamer. I shall never forget the rapture experienced by the doctor during this passage. On either hand the Alps towered upwards till they met the clouds, which were parted ever and anon, revealing to us a rich ethereal blue, pure as the dome of the poet's heaven. The mountain peaks were robed with snow, and with a blaze of glory glistened as the morning sun broke through the clouds. The hill-sides teemed with life and verdure, while the peasants, men and women, labouring with equal zeal, gathered their crops of hay, or tilled the willing soil, on slopes of green, by babbling brooks that glided adown the verdant glens, bearing on their bosom a sweet song to us in the stilly morn. There was no city with its din of industry, and dusty air, but up the mountain sides full many a village stood, whose church spires pointed to the way we think our spirits go. Here was summer, here was winter, here was spring and harvest time,—and here it was revealed to us, as though the Paradise of God had been unveiled, what beautiful combinations the Divine Mind is capable of arranging for our delight, and we instinctively asked, if these things we see with our eyes are so lovely, what must be the beauty of those riches prepared for us, which it hath not entered into the heart of man to conceive? So much were we entranced by the scenery, that we decided to break our journey at Giessbach, where we could enjoy almost absolute retirement, and regale ourselves nightly, viewing the unsurpassed brilliancy of the illuminated waterfall that rushes down a decline of nearly a thousand feet.

While we were reposing at this mountain retreat, the doctor suggested that our time be improved by recounting the story of the work done in London by the Jubilee Singers.

"That work," I said, "assumed a very interesting character from the outset; everything was new and untried. We had a most valuable introduction, but in a great city events crowd so closely upon one another; one must be quite alive to the advantages of the moment, or his opportunity will pass by, and some other attraction takes up the public attention. No mission like ours had ever, to my knowledge, been embarked upon British sympathies, and we were at a loss to know how the people would be most pleased to extend their co-operation. We could give our services in chapels, and take collections, but if this course were pursued, the chapels would be crowded by vast throngs of people, many of whom would have but little to give, and nothing would be assured. This plan was strongly recommended, but our American experience did not incline us to hope very largely for much success in this method of work. Another project was to give our concerts in halls almost exclusively, and charge an admission; but we were more especially dependent upon the religious portion of the community, and they were not all accustomed to attend concerts in halls; indeed, the idea of a concert to some minds was associated either with vulgar or debasing influences. We had been obliged from the first to depend largely upon people who were not accustomed to go out to evening gatherings, unless for some special religious service, at which they were admitted without entrance-fee. Some people from all classes were necessary in order to give complete success. We found that at many churches the people had never granted the use of their building for any gathering at which an admission-fee was charged; so that the doors were closed against us; and when chapels were granted us, the habits of the different religious bodies were such that persons of one denomination could not be counted upon to attend a gathering held in the church of any other; and besides this, when the service was given it was considered somewhat of an affair of that particular church, and not of the general public, and this had also to be taken into consideration. The clergymen of the Established Church would not feel at liberty to grant the use of their edifices. We knew, however, that they had much sympathy with our enterprise, and that we must devise some means to reap the benefit of it. Taking all things into consideration, I had believed from the first that, if we were to achieve distinguished success, our meetings must be held on neutral ground, and a charge made, and the co-operation of the whole community secured. But this plan for promoting benevolent enterprises was not sufficiently in vogue to insure the success of it from the outset.

"One of our earliest meetings was held in Union Chapel, Islington, of which the Rev. H. Allon, D.D., is the distinguished pastor. He hit upon the idea of holding a species of private concert, inviting people to attend by cards, upon which it should be stated that a collection would be made. By this means the families in the neighbourhood belonging to different religious societies could be gathered. On the announcement that a meeting would be held for the purpose of aiding the mission of the Jubilee Singers, and that people would be invited whose willingness and ability to aid missions were well known, it could also be announced that if any person wished to help the enterprise cards could be procured by application to the officer of the church. By this means a select audience was secured, every one of whom felt in honour bound to make a contribution. If our company had not been so large, or if we had not been in such haste to accomplish the object of our visit to England, I am confident that we might have accomplished very much good, and indeed that it would have been the best way to have promoted the mission work the Jubilee Singers represented; but the company was not organized and trained for this method of service, and reconstruction so far from home was not expedient, and besides, it was not always easy to find pastors who were willing to take the responsibility of extending the invitations. The Service of Song at Dr. Allon's was a most gratifying success, as the following extract abundantly indicates :—

"'10, *St. Mary's Road, Canonbury,*
"'*London, July* 13*th,* 1873.

"'MY DEAR MR. BEECHER,—

\* \* \* \* \* \*

I opened to them my chapel, to which gratuitous admission by tickets was given. The desire to hear them was so great that three times the number of tickets printed were applied for. There was a great and most enthusiastic crowd. The collection produced about £80. Since then the interest in them has been growing, and they will certainly have a hearty reception now that they are about to visit the provincial cities and towns of the kingdom. Their songs produce a strange weird effect. Notwithstanding the occasional dash of negro familiarity and quaintness of expression, they are full of religious earnestness and pathos, and one loses all sense of oddity in the feeling of real and natural piety. It will greatly help them that their performance is such as the most fastidious will not hesitate to welcome in our churches.

"' Affectionately yours,
"' HENRY ALLON.

"' *Rev. H. W. Beecher.*'

"The value of the good opinion of the singers entertained by Dr. Allon, will be best appreciated by those who are familiar with his musical publications, and his high standing among the Independents. His interest in us did not cease with the concert given at his church. From the first he indulged the idea that it would be much for the singers' advantage to appear at the annual dinner *conversazione* of the Congregational Union. On this occasion we should be sure to meet the leading men of the body, from all parts of the kingdom, and after the repast was over they would be in the best possible mood for hearing a few songs. Accordingly, through the politeness of the Rev. A. Hannay, tickets for the company were secured and a programme made for the occasion.

"These annual gatherings of the Congregational Union are of an eminently social character; from the hard taxing work of hearing and making reports and addresses relating to the business and prospects of the work done by the denomination during the anniversaries, the ministers and delegates relax themselves at the dinner, and indulge in such social communion as helps to cement the bonds of fellowship, dear to all Christian workers. The chairman of the Union, who holds his office for a year, presides on this occasion, and I make no doubt indulges in his choicest veins of humour to give relish to the repast, and the 'flow of soul' carries on its tide the 'feast of reason,' as little boats dance on the tiny bosom of a garden lake. Many good thoughts would lie stranded for ever were it not for the hilarity occasioned by a good dinner. In London these social gatherings are held in the large hall at the Cannon Street Terminus Hotel, which will accommodate about seven hundred persons. The day the singers were there the room was densely crowded; they occupied a small balcony at the end opposite the chairman, while I was honoured with a seat near him, to watch the course of events. Dr. Allon was near, and having served as chairman one year, was competent to secure any attentions for us that might otherwise have been missed in the hilarious confusion incident to an occasion not arranged for any methodical business. The Rev. Eustace Conder, M.A., was in the chair; the Rev. Dr. Raleigh was near, and having heard the singers at Willis's Rooms, glowed with zeal to have them appreciated by the company; while Mr. Hannay and many others were not slow to prepare a way for their introduction. When the time came for the singing, the chairman, in his kindly way, introduced the singers, who rendered one of their best pieces, to the great delight of the brethren. I have always found that, on the one hand, no company of men are more elastic, explosive, merry, and happy than a company of divines on a festive occasion; and why should it not be so? 'How beautiful are the feet of those who bring good tidings and publish peace;' why should they not be among the happiest? On the other hand, I have noticed that the slave songs, born of religious devotion, express a heart language, recognised instantly by pious people who think much of the blessings of salvation. So when the Jubilee Singers sang, 'Oh, brothers, don't—stay away, for the Bible says there's room enough,' they only went on to preach what the minister had been doing for years. When they broke forth, 'There are Angels hovering round, to carry the tidings home,' 'oh,' say the preachers, 'we have been trying to comfort our people with these stories of ministering spirits'; and when again they sang, 'Preachers, don't grow weary, for your work is almost done,' the song came home like a heavenly breeze, to regale the heart and to urge the weary brain on till solaced to believe that other word of consolation the Jubilee Singers brought, 'Wait a little while, and we'll sing the new song.' I really think the students never appeared before a body of men in Great Britain who had such ability to appreciate their songs as the ministers and delegates at the Congregational Union dinner; because the body was so representative of a particular class of men. The applause was so hearty, I fear the brethren might think me discourteous if I should make known to the public how enthusiastic it was. Nothing bore them up on loftier wings than the singing of the 'John Brown' song. Something better than dull hard grinding work is the sometime portion of the servants of God. Speeches were made, and one other inevitable thing,—I mean a collection. Goodness must give, pious emotions must express themselves by an offering. When you touch the vein of a person, if the blood does not flow, the person is dead; when you touch the soul, lit by a holy fire, born of another world, and destined for his father's house, the soul gives of its life, its preciousness, its fragrance, that lessens not while it imparts. If there be no giving either in substance or purpose, the soul is dead. The contribution at this time was liberal, and the promises of co-operation many, and very serviceable to us later on in the campaign. Another work performed about this time was in connection with the annual meeting of the Freedmen's Mission Aid Society. This society is an auxiliary to the American Missionary Association, established mainly through the exertions of the Rev. J. W. Healy, D.D., to secure the co-operation of the British public with Christians in America in efforts for the evangelization of the African race; it had been in operation but a year, nevertheless its success had been very encouraging, and more than £7,000 promised for its work. Great efforts were put forth to make its first anniversary meeting a success. A proper programme was prepared and cards of invitation sent to a large number of representative people. The fact that the Jubilee Singers were to be present was a great inducement for many to attend. The fine hall with its anterooms were literally packed long before the hour announced for the commencement of the meeting, and hundreds had to be turned away  Lord Shaftesbury occupied the chair, and was supported by the Hon. Arthur Kinnaird, M.P., Treasurer of the society, the Revs. Mr. Moffat (from South Africa), and Newman Hall, with others. The Rev. L. D. Bevan, the Hon. Secretary, read the report. For three hundred years, it was said, the whites had sought to evangelize Africa, but had failed, on account of obstacles presented by climate, customs, and so forth; but now the hope was in the American Freedman, that he should become educated, and evangelize his fatherland. At the conclusion Lord Shaftesbury called upon the singers to render, 'Oh how I love Jesus!' when they received a hearty welcome. Perhaps the most significant address was made by the Rev. J. S. Moffat, the brother-in-law of Livingstone. He told how he had come home from Africa the year before in profound depression, 'home from holding his tiny rushlight amidst the desolations of that continent, and holding it with the feeling that his efforts were almost futile. His station was a thousand miles inland, and yet he might stand on the hill and look right away, to the Atlantic in one direction, to the Indian Ocean in the other, and also far away to the northward, and feel that there was not another Christian Missionary to be found in the immense area. When he stood there, with heathenism on every side, no wonder perhaps he sometimes felt cast down; but, looking at the Jubilee Singers, he could see where light and hope were to come. It was utterly useless, humanly speaking, for us, alone, to seek to evangelize Africa, but in the trained members of the African race we might look for glorious fruits.' At the close the singers sang, 'Go down Moses, way down in Egypt land, tell ole Pharaoh, let my people go,' which, after Mr. Moffat's speech, was very effective. There was present the Rev. W. C. Van Meter, the founder of the home for little wanderers in New York City. As this Christian brother had had much experience in raising money at meetings where his little wanderers sang, and as he had lived among slaveholders in America, and subsequently laboured for the elevation of the Freedmen, he was in every way at home when his turn came to address the audience. He told of the suffering he had seen—he told of prophetic utterances of Christian negroes long before the war of emancipation, which revealed how certain it was that God assured the hearts of these people that, at some day, they should be free. As was happily said by a reporter present, 'Mr. Van Meter spoke with an energy and naturalness that lashed the audience into a perfect storm of enthusiasm, so that when the cheering subsided, and the singers arose and gave the famous "John Brown" song, the sight was such as we have not witnessed in London for many years. As the refrain rang out, "John Brown died, that the slave might be free," the dense audience could suppress their feelings no longer; they rose from their seats, and their applause was deafening, hats and handkerchiefs were waved, and the excitement continued until "God save the Queen" was sung.' The Rev. Dr. Healy and Dr. Waddington followed with addresses. The Rev. Newman Hall made some felicitous remarks, and from that hour manifested the most kindly interest in the mission of the singers. Lord Shaftesbury declared to the audience that he always loved the negro, and that the chanting of 'The Lord's Prayer' was one of the most beautiful things he ever heard in his life, and that he wished it repeated. 'And thus closed,' said *The Baptist*, in its excellent report, 'one of the most successful gatherings of the year.'

"In America the Jubilee Singers frequently appeared at Sabbath services, and sang in the place of the choir, or held a missionary meeting in place of the ordinary service. I had expected that we might accomplish much good work this way in England; but it was found that the habits of English Nonconformists respecting these services are different from the American churches. The Dissenters confine themselves mostly to congregational singing, and to allow the singers to appear and render music with which the congregation was not familiar would be looked upon as a species of exhibition that would be questionable. This kind of exhibition, however, was for the promotion of the interests of the mission of the Jubilee Singers, in which we believed, and therefore hailed with pleasure any opportunity of establishing a precedent in our favour. During the six weeks I had spent in London there was nothing to encourage me in the belief that as missionary workers there would be duties for us on the Lord's day, which, to one who had been accustomed to do most of his work on the Sabbath, was somewhat trying. When, therefore, Newman Hall asked if the singers could be present at Surrey Chapel and sing in connection with his Sabbath service, we were much encouraged. His plan was this: the singers were to be seated near the pulpit; he would preach for a little while on the bondage and deliverance of the Children of Israel, after which the students were to sing, 'Go down Moses'; then he would preach of Christ, another great Deliverer, when the singers were to follow with, 'Oh how I love Jesus.' No mention was to be made of the fact that the singers were to be present at this service.

"The morning came, everything was auspicious, and members of Surrey Chapel, who had prayed for many years for the emancipation of the American slave, and, during the war, for the success of the Northern armies, rejoiced as those whose prayers had been answered. We were all hailed as genuine missionaries, doing a work eminently fitting for the Lord's day, and, so far as I know, the Rev. Newman Hall had the praise and approbation of all his people in this act of welcome to the Jubilee Singers. This Sabbath service, however, was not all the experience we were to have at the chapel made famous by the labours of Rowland Hill, and his equally renowned successor. Newman Hall proposed that we should give a concert, and charge an admission fee. His proposition was gladly accepted, and no pains were spared by him or the associate pastor of the church in making known our mission and in encouraging the people to patronise it. Many distinguished persons were present among the crowded audience that greeted the singers on the night of the concert; and among the number the Rev. Dr. Lindsley, an American missionary, who had laboured many years among the Zulus in Southern Africa. Nothing seemed to me more encouraging than the enthusiasm with which missionaries who had spent many years in Africa ever manifested for the Jubilee Singers. These men, who have long toiled and reflected much respecting the conversion of a people in a land almost impenetrable to the white man, have great faith in the ability of the American Freedmen to penetrate and evangelize Africa; as these emancipated ones become educated, they rise up as morning stars before the missionaries, to usher in a millennial day for their fatherland. Again, I have noticed that the veteran missionary is always overjoyed to have a sympathy awakened in behalf of the people for whom he has been labouring. The venerable Dr. Moffat never met the Jubilee Singers without feeling that his heart was young again. They brought to him hope for their people, and a zeal to renew the labours he entered upon more than fifty years ago. A concert of the singers was always a thanksgiving day to all such men. The concert at Surrey Chapel was very well received; Mr. Hall was in his happiest mood, and took occasion to introduce an exhortation on beneficence and temperance as well, stating that he was able to preach on so many different occasions because he was a teetotaller. During these days the Jubilee Singers were giving concerts in different halls and chapels with moderate success. At the Hanover Square Rooms and St. James's Large Hall many acquaintances were formed, but the great expenses attending concerts in those places nearly equalled the receipts. There were many ministers who offered us the use of their chapels, with the promise of assistance in providing for the details of the service. Among the invitations of this kind that were accepted was one from the Rev. J. G. Rogers, the present chairman of the Congregational Union; one from the Rev. T. W. Aveling, of Kingsland Chapel; the Rev. Dr. Edmonds, Presbyterian minister; and the Rev. Vincent Tymms, a Baptist minister, Lower Clapton. These, as with others, were well attended and accompanied with financial success. The ability of the English people to 'be given to hospitality' is, I believe, superior to that of any other nation; I think it is a national instinct: when, therefore, a religious society invited us to their chapel, they all felt an enthusiasm to see us entertained, and this alone was sufficient to insure some financial success.

"The American Missionary Association, in its evangelistic work, always set its standard of morality and conduct very high: it was anti-slavery, anti-caste, anti-rum, anti-tobacco. It is contrary to its principles to employ persons who use either alcoholic drinks or tobacco as a stimulant; and the Fisk University is especially rigid respecting all such things. We found, therefore, that the National Temperance League looked upon the Jubilee Singers, from the first, as allies, and hailed their appearance with joy. The Rev. Mr. Rae, their energetic secretary, manifested no lack of interest in securing their attendance at the soirée of the National Temperance League at the Cannon Street Terminus Hotel. This body of workers are persistent and kindly in their labour. When I am told that in this climate people need stimulants more than in America, I always think of Newman Hall, Mr. Rae, and John M. Cook, the excursionist, who travels with personally-conducted parties to the ends of the earth, and who told me that he never tasted a drop of liquor in his life. If any healthier-looking people can be found on the face of the globe than those who formed the company at the National Temperance Soirée, I have yet to see them. People from all classes were present, and joy and gladness filled the place. Mr. Thomas Cook, the senior excursionist, delivered an address on 'All round the World.' A programme, including music by distinguished artists, was introduced, and the first part of it performed. 'Then,' says the *Temperance Record,* 'the platform was cleared for the Jubilee Minstrels: the melodies they sang were not more touching to the tender-hearted than they were delightful to the musical *connoisseur;* so popular were the minstrels, that the second part of the musical programme, in which the first-named *artistes* were to have taken part, had to be eliminated, and the meeting which followed was also curtailed.' The Quakers present seemed entirely willing that the singers should recite their poetry in their own peculiar way. The servants crowded the passage ways. 'Every ear,' says the *Christian World,* 'was strained to catch the liquid melody that now came hushed and gentle as the soft sigh of a summer night, and anon thundered along clear and loud as a clarion call to victory and joy.' But the temperance people did not exhaust their interest by the welcome given on this occasion, though a collection was added to the entertainment. A great annual fête was to be held at the Crystal Palace in July, and the use of the Opera Hall was tendered the singers free of charge; this was not only a concession on the part of the temperance people, but also of the managers of the Crystal Palace, who relinquished the *pro rata* charge allowed them on the number of attendants. All the advertising was done in a thorough manner by the Temperance committee, without expense to the Jubilee Singers. The day was exceedingly warm, and the movements of the vast crowd about the Palace unfavourable for the effects of much of the singing; but the audience was most generous and sympathetic, and Mr. Bowly, president of the League, manifested the kindliest interest in the mission. The great event of this occasion was reserved for the vast central transept. Five thousand children were seated upon the orchestra, conducted under the able management of Mr. Frederic Smith. It was a grand sight to see this temperance army, and to hear them render their songs with a precision of time, and excellency of taste, that spoke volumes in praise of their leader. The crowds of people were simply immense. It occurred to some of us that, although the Jubilee Singers might not be heard to great advantage in so large an audience room, nevertheless, the thousands of children and the older representatives from the length and breadth of the country would obtain an idea of their mission, and possibly a lasting interest in the African race, if they came on the orchestra and sang two or three songs. 'One of them,' says the *Daily News*, 'was the song of emancipation, "John Brown's body," and at the last verse Mr. F. Smith, the talented conductor, rapped up his well-disciplined army of choristers, who thundered forth the chorus with all the more zest because it was impromptu. The enthusiasm which followed this was very remarkable. At least ten thousand persons leaped to their feet, shouted, waved their hats and handkerchiefs, and made the roof echo with round after round of applause.' The *Temperance Record* gives the following notice :—

"'Then notably there was the concert of the Jubilee Singers. Did Longfellow know of their singing or their coming? Surely he did when he wrote the poem of the slave singing at midnight.

"'Loud he sang the Psalm of David!
He, a negro and enslavèd,
Sang of Israel's victory,
Sang of Zion, bright and free.

And the voice of his devotion
Filled my soul with strange emotion;
For its tones by turns were glad,
Sweetly solemn, wildly sad.

"'Longfellow must have prophetically beheld the temperance fête of 1873. How his heart would leap up could he have heard the sable offshoots of slavery, slaves no more, mingling their voices with the blue-eyed, fair-haired Saxons!'

"Never in England was it the lot of the Jubilee Singers to cast themselves upon the mercy of so vast a throng of sympathetic fellow-workers, for the amelioration of the condition of the common people, and never was their mission of love better blessed than by the great cold water army, that shall yet do, under

Providence, as vast a work in emancipating the English poor from the evils of strong drink as the armies of the North had done for the breaking of the chains of the Jubilee Singers and the people they represented in America."

## CHAPTER V.

### HOSPITALITIES RECEIVED IN LONDON.

AFTER our delightful rest at Giessbach, the doctor and I proceeded over the Brunic Pass of the Alps, watching for long hours the thread of the river Aar, that coursed in silvery beauty along the bosom of the vale at the foot of the mountains. We did not purpose to break our journey at Lucerne, except for the Sabbath, as our chief interest on this portion of our route was centred on the Evangelical Missionary College at Bâle, on the banks of the Rhine. The doctor had learned that this institution furnished many missionaries for Africa, and was anxious to inform himself fully concerning the details of its work. On our arrival one of the professors took us through the building, and gave us information about its history and methods. We learned that the seminary was opened in 1816, and that it depended upon annual subscriptions for the furtherance of its designs. Last year the professor said the expenditure of the society to which the college belongs amounted to about £40,000 or $200,000. I also learned the number of students educated for Christian work had been nine hundred and fifty-six, the number sent to Africa ninety-nine, and the number of converts on the Gold Coast of Africa, where their missions were established, two thousand four hundred and fourteen. It was their purpose to extend these missions to the kingdom of Ashantee. Neither the graduates of this seminary nor the society to which it belongs are pledged to labour in any particular country. Their field is the world, and they have missions in China, East India, and Persia, as well as in Africa, while many of their students have entered into the labours of other missionary societies in Russia, Turkey, Australia, also in North and South America. "This college," said the doctor afterwards to me, "is the sunniest spot on the continent; the best evidence I have seen that God has not given the people over to the devices of Roman Catholicism." From its hallowed grounds we repaired across the Rhine, to some German hills that towered in the distance, after which I went on to give the story of some of the kindnesses bestowed upon the Jubilee Singers on their arrival in England.

"The hospitalities we received in London," I said, "were among the golden events of our lives. No youths from America ever had such honours from the English people as the Jubilee Singers. Hospitality is one of the embellishments of philanthropy; it is the flower and sweetness of friendship. I never observed anything so kingly in a householder as his cheery cordiality and joy at seeing his guests happy; he who is giving a welcome and entertainment to messengers of good is but reflecting the spirit of Him who shall come with all His holy angels by-and-by to welcome us to the great marriage supper; and those who minister on such occasions are learning to do as angels do. Hospitality is a refreshment, not a service; it is no teacher of dogmas, it makes no provision for exhortation or precept, it comes upon the soul like the dew of Hermon, the Sun of righteousness shines upon it, and as the morning sun gathers the drops of dew and weaves a veil of fleecy clouds for her noonday adorning, so 'our Light,' when *He* shall come, will be bedecked with clouds. 'Be not forgetful to entertain strangers' is not apt to be forgotten, when they can sing. Perhaps the people think them the 'angels unawares.'

"Singing praises to God is the flying of the soul on angels' wings. Who has not been 'caught up in the air' by 'psalms and hymns and spiritual songs'? And who shall say we may not, in the last times, be flooded above the perishing world by a tide of angels' songs?

"Hospitality is not merely the outgrowth of religion, it is the fruit of culture and wealth as well. A broad cultivated heart always has room in it to spare. The guests of the great and good are as essential to their completeness as paintings and statuary. No right-minded man plans for himself a mansion without making generous provision for the accommodation of friends,—servants and horses even are secured,—with reference to the exigences of hospitality. There are, moreover, seasons in the histories of nations and men; new countries indulge in freshness and budding hopes; then comes summer and sometime harvest. This latter season is upon the English people; they are rich, they are learned, they are Christian, and ripe for every good word and work, they are 'given to hospitality.' Among the foremost of this class are the members of the Society of Friends; as their names suggest, so their deeds attest. To be a friend, the friend of the poor and oppressed, is the normal business of a Quaker, and no regalia of office ever seems more royal to me than a Quaker bonnet. It signifies that the possessor is an office-bearer of King Emmanuel; when she goes about the streets I always feel that some one is out on the King's business. Society cannot afford to have the Friends drop the name of Quaker; it is as surely a wealth in the galaxy of the great and good as the name of Raphael among the family of painters. I have always taken it for granted when meeting a Quaker that my errand needed no elaborate explanation; I expected that he was ready for it.

"Before we reached England Mr. Stafford Allen had sent £20 for the Fisk University, and having, while in America, visited that institution, he was able at once to commend the Jubilee Singers to his friends. The Rev. Mr. Powell, my associate at that time, made his acquaintance, and an interest was awakened that spread among the Quakers throughout the kingdom. It was not long before Mr. Samuel Gurney, formerly member of Parliament, sought us out, and invited us to his spacious mansion on the confines of Regent's Park. As Mr. Gurney was a very prominent member of the Society of Friends, we anticipated meeting at his house persons who would gladly render us much aid in our enterprise. It was a lovely day when we met him by appointment to accept his guidance through the Botanical and Zoological Gardens, prior to the welcome that awaited us at his residence. I shall never forget the hearty reception he gave the singers, and the wonder we all experienced at the attractions of the Regent's Park. To an American, and especially to one who has lived in New York, it is a constant surprise to find so much open ground in London. The system of parks gives one the idea that land is almost as free and abundant as the air. The poorest can roam on a holiday or an evening through broad acres of open ground beneath the spreading boughs of trees, and by artificial lakes, or jetting fountains. He may seat himself in the cool shade on easy benches, provided either by Government or charity, and feel amid the freshness and beauty of the country, even in the heart of the great metropolis of the world; such are the possibilities of an inland city, whose suburbs may be made co-extensive with the whole country. Mr. Gurney kindly conducted the singers first through the Zoological Gardens, and took pains to reach the abode of the lions at four o'clock, that the students might see them partake of their dinner. There was something about the savage eagerness of these wild beasts in seizing their food that almost put to the blush one who had so often taken his dinner at a New York eating-house; the genuine lion has even more avidity than the commercial one.

"The advantages of the Londoners in sustaining these gardens are great; their climate is neither excessively hot nor cold; the polar bear can endure the heat, and the Indian elephant the cold. The hippopotamus can roll in his open bath in the midst of winter, and birds and reptiles, even from the centre of Africa, thrive and multiply. I remember, however, that we were shown a species of ape, kept in a heated room. When we entered, the ape shook us by the hand, and looked at us with a mute intelligence; he opened and closed the doors for visitors, and exhibited many evidences of training. A shudder passed over me as though the soul of man had been confined in the body of a beast. It was terribly suggestive of Darwinism, and I fled from its presence, and banished its form from my mind, as I would an apparition

"Mr. Gurney kindly told us much about the Botanical Gardens, as he led us into the midst of their flowery walks, and arbours of leafy freshness. The singers had never witnessed anything so complete of its kind; and its oceans of flowers, arranged in billows of beauty, captivated with delight the attention of every one of us. Little did Mr. Gurney know how 'he led us through the green pastures, and beside the still waters, restoring our souls'—that day. On reaching his home, after a stroll of several hours, we found his family and friends gathered in a Paradise of their own. The trees, and vines, and flowery walks, possible in England on account of the evenness and humidity of the temperature, are not possible in America. When I have roamed over them in the semi-secluded gardens of the rich and noble, I have been fain to ask, what better can be ours on the bank of the river, 'midst the Trees of Life, with their various fruits, and birds, and songs of the Redeemed? Aye, more,—I have thought the promise of these things that have come down to us gave the model, so that these earthly scenes are but a foretaste of things heavenly, the Beulah grounds, where we may breathe, for a little, in the anticipations of the Paradise of God. Mrs. Gurney had provided tables in sheltered places in the garden and conservatories sufficient for the accommodation of about one hundred persons. The intercourse with the family and visitors was delightful; there is a charm in being served by the hands of kindness and refinement. He who has experienced the ministration of a loving and intelligent mother, has been blessed with a quality of grace such as no menial servant can bestow. I have ever felt the riches of this grace shed upon me whenever partaking of the hospitality of the Quakers in company with the Jubilee Singers. After the repast was over, we repaired to spacious rooms, and the evening was occupied in conversation with those who, for many years, had yearned and toiled for the abolition of slavery the world around. As I remember the happy countenances of the aged people, and think of their emotions and tears, when the songs of the singers rang cheerily through the halls, or sank in soft cadences and touched the soul like a gentle summer's breeze; when I think of the hieroglyphics of peace and joy that were seen even on the wrinkles of age; when I recall the words spoken of triumph, I have a vision of those who shall meet on the other shore the redeemed of the Lord returning with singing unto Zion; it is of those who shall meet the very ones who have been emancipated from sin, partially by their own labours. There is something money cannot buy. I saw it that night,—it was the blessedness experienced by veteran Friends, who witnessed, in the Jubilee Singers, the triumphs of faith, and sacrifice offered in years gone by. As the rich tide of reflections rolled over their souls, bearing on its bosom many precious memories, something told me, as if an angel spoke, 'Their works do follow them.' All their acts were tenderness, and all their deeds were love. And when we parted from the company,' midst an ocean of benedictions, we felt crowned for our work and reward. We had many invitations to private families about this time, but could accept few. One, however, from Mr. George McDonald, has an especial claim for notice. This distinguished author, after having heard the singers in New York, said of them in his letter to Dr. Allon:—

" 'There is something inexpressibly touching in their wonderfully sweet, round, bell voice, in the way in which they sing—so artless in its art yet so consummate in expression—and in the mingling of the pathetic with the unconscious comic in the rude hymns, shot here and there with a genuine thread of poetry. I feel confident they will make a great impression in many religious circles.'

"By this he evinced that they would promote religious work. It was very natural, therefore, for him, when he made his annual feast, inviting the poor, to seek the services of the singers for the benefit of his guests. Everything was very appropriate. Mr. McDonald's 'retreat,' on the banks of the Thames, affords ample grounds for a large garden party; his happy family gladly prepared themselves to perform a simple play of an elevating character written by Mrs. McDonald for the occasion. A stage was constructed in the garden. All the people from some wretched street in the densely-populated metropolis were invited, and conveyed in waggons to the spot where they were made as happy as possible. The singers chanted the 'Lord's Prayer' before the curtain was raised for the play, and rendered several of their songs during the visit. The entertainment afforded very much gratification. Never have I so fully realized the blessedness of the Saviour's words, 'But when thou makest a feast, call the poor, the maimed, the lame, the blind, and thou shalt be blessed; for they cannot recompense thee: for thou shalt be recompensed at the resurrection of the just.'

"Mrs. McDonald informed me that during the seven years since they instituted these garden parties, she had witnessed very great improvement in the character of the visitors; taken as they were from the slums of vice and poverty, many were unacquainted even with the ordinary use of the conveniences of table service; but by the kind attentions of other guests always present, and by the object-lessons afforded to the happy observers, wonders had been wrought. Mr. White and the Jubilee Singers were in their element, and never was a more grateful service rendered in England. When one person rises from want and obscurity he teaches others how to rise. When one goes down into low places and leads others to a higher elevation, rescuing them from penury and making them rich with the love of God, he wins his title of 'joint-heir with Christ.' Of Mr. George McDonald, the author of 'Robert Falkner,' it can truly be said, 'He hath dispersed, he hath given to the poor, his horn shall be exalted with honour;' and when I think of his residence on the peaceful banks of the Thames, Isaiah speaks to me, 'If thou draw out thy soul to the hungry, and satisfy the afflicted soul, thou shalt be as a watered garden, and as springs of water, whose waters fail not.' And when I have sat with Mr. McDonald amidst his happy family, how deeply have I felt, 'Blessed is he that considereth the poor; he shall be blessed upon the earth.' There are ever fountains by our side from whence we may drink of the water He shall give who says, 'He that giveth to the poor shall not lack;' and again, 'He that hath pity on the poor lendeth to the Lord, and that he hath given will He pay him again.' 'The poor ye have always with you.' God's bank is near our door, and we may deposit our money in it any day, and the interest will be 'some thirty, some sixty, and some one hundred fold.'

The most distinguished invitation, however, bestowed upon us came through the kind consideration of the Rev. Newman Hall, on the occasion of the laying of the foundation stone of Christ's Church, which his congregation are rearing to perpetuate the name and work of Rowland Hill. Mr. Hall remarked to me that he had that morning taken breakfast with Mrs.

Gladstone, and had mentioned the Jubilee Singers to her incidentally. She expressed to him, he said, a desire that they should come to her house. I begged him to inform her that it would give us the greatest pleasure to visit her residence on any occasion. After waiting a week or more, I began to fear that nothing immediate was likely to come from his communication with Mrs. Gladstone. In a day or two word was sent to Mr. Powell that Mrs. Gladstone wished to see him at once, at Carlton House Terrace, to make some arrangements respecting the appearance of the Jubilee Singers at a lunch, which was to be given to the Prince and Princess of Wales, and others of the Royal Family. It is hardly necessary to say that the invitation was accepted with the utmost thankfulness.

"Mrs. Gladstone's purpose was that the singers should chant the 'Lord's Prayer' as a grace before lunch, and render any other service that might be desirable during the stay of the royal guests. Good fortune seemed to take the singers on its wings, and the most desirable circumstances, like favouring gales, wafted them on. For the glory of God it should be said that, through all these days and nights, very many earnest prayers were offered up that *He* would show us the right way that we might walk therein. There were many hedges set about us, as well as distracting incompatibilities. To scale the Alpine heights of society needs much of the consecration of a soldier: and when the business is for Christ's sake, the Holy Ghost must help our infirmities. I think it was with feelings and experiences like these that many of us appeared at Mr. Gladstone's on the occasion of the lunch given to the Prince. We arrived in good time, and received every attention requisite for our ease and comfort. The royal guests consisted of the following distinguished persons and others: their Royal Highnesses the Prince and Princess of Wales, accompanied by Her Imperial Highness the Grand Duchess Czarevna, His Royal Highness the Duke of Cambridge, His Excellency Count Beust, the Duke and Duchess of Buccleuch, the Duke of Sutherland, Earl Granville, the Countess Spencer, the Bishop of Winchester, the Right Hon. John Bright, and Mr. Motley.

"Luncheon was served in the dining-room, covers being laid for twenty-four. Near the entrance to the room there are alcoves on either side: in one of these the singers were stationed when the royal party passed. The Prince of Wales was accompanied by Mrs. Gladstone, while the Princess leaned on the Premier's arm. As soon as they were seated at the table, according to arrangement, the students chanted the 'Lord's Prayer.' Standing in the alcove as they did, I think they had not been observed by many of the party, who seemed a little surprised and uncertain as to the source of the music. It was not long, however, before everything was explained by one and another, and more singing was requested. With other pieces, the 'John Brown' song was sung, with all the soul and power usually thrown into it by the singers: nothing had pleased the Royal party so well. The Prince of Wales looked over the book containing the history of the singers and their songs, and asked for 'No more auction-block for me,' which seemed to give him much satisfaction. Nothing, however, awakened such enthusiasm as 'John Brown,' and Mr. Gladstone asked me if it could not be repeated as a special favour to the Grand Duchess Czarevna, whose father-in-law had emancipated the serfs in Russia. Miss Sheppard, who acted as leader in Mr. White's absence, complied, with her usual propriety. At three o'clock a select company assembled to meet their Royal Highnesses: there were in the party, His Excellency Count Munster, German ambassador; the Countess de Brunnow; the Duke and Duchess of Argyll and Lady Evelyn Campbell; the Earl and Countess of Stanhope; the Marquis and Marchioness del Grillo; Viscount and Viscountess Sydney; Lord Richard Cavendish, General the Right Hon. Sir William Knollys, Mr. Goldschmidt and his distinguished consort Jenny Lind, and others. The Princess of Wales and the Czarevna took unusual interest in some of the singers, and inquired of them concerning their history, purposes, and success. Jenny Lind

# HOSPITALITIES RECEIVED IN LONDON. 77

honoured them all by some word of encouragement; while John Bright and the late Bishop of Winchester manifested an interest full of the tenderest emotions. We did not know at the time that the Bishop of Winchester was a son of the Great Wilberforce, and one of the most eloquent men in the country: his accidental death a few days afterwards threw a flood of light on his worth and works, and illustrated how a wise Providence often times a good man's death so as to bring freshly to light the story of his life, as an example to the living. Before leaving, refreshments were served to the singers, and Mr. Motley, author of 'The Dutch Republic,' called me aside and begged me to accept a donation for the Fisk University.

"We now supposed that our highest fortune in this way was attained, but God had ordered it otherwise. A few days after I received the following note:—

"'11, *Carlton House Terrace.*

"'DEAR SIR,—

"'I beg you to accept the assurances of the great pleasure which the Jubilee Singers gave on Monday to our illustrious guests, and to all who heard them. I should wish to offer a little present in books in acknowledgment of their kindness, and in connection with the purposes, as they have been announced, of their visit to England. It has occurred to me that perhaps they might like to breakfast with us, my family and a very few friends, but I would not ask this unless it is thoroughly agreeable to them. With the singers, who, I believe, are eleven, we would, of course, hope to see you and Mr. White. I would propose Tuesday next, the 22nd, and ten as the time.

"'Believe me, dear Sir,

"'Your very faithful servant,

"'WM. E. GLADSTONE.

"'Rev. G. D. Pike.'

On reading it I was simply confounded. The past history of these people rushed over my mind. The times when accommodation had been refused both to my agents and myself at hotels flashed upon my memory a greater glare of ugliness than ever; the tedious days I had spent in getting them passage by steamer to this country looked to me like remnants of the dark ages. If the Prime Minister of England can ask coloured people to sit at his table, can we not hope our loved country, where all men are born free and equal, where there is no aristocracy, where 'high worth is elevated place,' will sit in sackcloth for the abominations she hath done, till her wicked prejudices are taken away? I have ever felt that this event was worth as much to the coloured people the world over as the campaign cost us; and after it had transpired, I knew that our mission could in no case be reckoned a failure. By reason of the death of the Bishop of Winchester the breakfast was deferred for a week later than the date fixed. Mr. White, the singers, and myself were able to meet the engagement. At the close of the interview Rev. Newman Hall and myself exchanged some thoughts about the contrast between this scene and those to which I have just alluded as occurring in America, and the great value to the colored people of a full account of these proceedings in some of the religious papers in our country. Much to my joy I afterwards saw the following communication in the *New York Independent* :—

"'MR. GLADSTONE AND THE JUBILEE SINGERS.

(BY THE REV. NEWMAN HALL.)

"'Our Jubilee friends will not soon forget the interesting breakfast party given yesterday by Mr. and Mrs. Gladstone, at their private residence on Carlton House Terrace, nor will those forget it who had the pleasure of meeting them there. They had already sung at the premier's in the presence of the Prince and Princess of Wales, the Czarowitz and the Czarevna, of Russia, the Right Hon. John Bright, and a distinguished party of nobility. But on that occasion they came to entertain the guests. Yesterday they were themselves the guests. I had feared that the party must have been put off, for I had just read in the *Daily News* that Mr. Gladstone was lying ill at Chiselhurst. But as I was at the door a carriage drove up, and Mr. and Mrs. Gladstone alighted. They had come up from Chiselhurst to meet their negro friends. Mr. Gladstone looked pale and worn. He had, by his physician's order, excused himself from attending the great banquet to be given that evening by the lord mayor to the ministry, at the Mansion House; and he might with great propriety have rested at Chiselhurst and put off his guests. But he rose early, travelled some twenty-five miles by rail, and then drove to his home, which he reached just before the Rev. Mr. Pike and the Jubilee Singers, and so in time to greet them.

"'Mr. Gladstone's town residence has a spacious entrance-hall, leading to a large dining-room, which overlooks St. James's Park, and opens upon a wide terrace. A front room is the premier's study. A wide double staircase leads to a suite of reception rooms, filled with rare, costly, and beautiful art treasures. There are paintings and sculptures by eminent artists, and cases filled with specimens of ceramic art of all ages. There are works by Cellini, and specimens of pottery collected during many years by one whose fame as a statesman and orator alone prevents his being famous in literature and art—spheres in which he has few rivals. Breakfast was laid in the dining-room, on tables beautifully decorated with flowers. In addition to the Jubilee party of fifteen, there were present Lord and Lady Cavendish, Lord Lyttleton, the Right Hon. W. E. Forster, M.P., Cabinet minister, the Hon. Arthur Kinnaird, M.P., the dean of the Queen's Chapel Royal, together with Mrs. Gladstone, two Misses Gladstone, Mr. W. H. Gladstone, M.P., and others. The guests were seated at two tables, our negro friends being equally distributed, sitting between their English friends. At the table where the dean and myself sat, Mrs. Gladstone, Miss Gladstone, and Mr. W. H. Gladstone were most assiduous in their kind attentions —not only seeing that the physical comfort of their negro guests was attended to, but conversing with them so constantly and pleasantly that they were quite at their ease. At the other table Lady Cavendish, acting for Mrs. Gladstone and seated side by side with her coloured sisters, diffused the same atmosphere of social geniality around. A number of liveried footmen ministered also to the wants of the guests, paying as much attention and deference to the coloured singers from Tennessee as to the titled ladies of the English aristocracy and to the untitled but no less noble lady whose guests we were. To English readers I should apologise for writing in this way. My description would be severely criticised, as giving prominence to trifling courtesies which with us are matters of course. No one here, pretending to social refinement, would make the least distinction between the guests he might meet merely on the ground of colour, and no one would hesitate on that account to invite to his house any one otherwise suitable. I am told that there still exists in the United States some remnant of the old prejudice. This may be found, no doubt, amongst some of the ignorant and vulgar of our own land; and so also it would not be fair to infer that such prejudice is general in America because exhibited by some low-bred, unrefined, and narrow souls. I fancy some of these were at Surrey Chapel the other Sunday morning, when the Jubilee Singers did me the honour of taking a little luncheon with some of my friends at Rowland Hill's parsonage. Some Americans had come to take my hand, and I asked them to join us. But when they entered the house, and saw our negro friends sitting down to table side by side with some English ladies, they looked surprised, stood awhile at the door, and then walked away down the street! I wish they had been present yesterday to see Mrs. Gladstone and her daughters, and the noble lords and ladies present, taking their negro friends by the hand, placing them chairs, sitting at their side, pouring out their tea, etc., and conversing with them in a manner utterly free from any approach either to pride or condescension ; but exactly as if they had been white people in their own rank of life. And this not as an effort, nor for the show of it, but from a habit of social intercourse which would have rendered any other conduct perfectly impossible.

"'Mr. Gladstone charmed us with his eloquent description of a book on the Modoc Indians he had just been reading, making one marvel how, with all his great cares of state and Parliament, he can find time, as he does, to keep ever abreast of the literature of the day. After breakfast he showed to his guests some of the principal objects of interest in his collection of art treasures, explaining them in his own fascinating style. Then, all the party being gathered in the drawing-room, the Jubilee Singers entertained us with their wonderful music. First we had "John Brown." I never heard them sing it as they did yesterday. It was not the music alone, but the features of the singers also which made it so impressive. They sang as beings inspired. Their whole forms seemed to dilate. Their eyes flashed ; their countenances told of reverence and joy and gratitude to God. Never shall I forget Mr. Gladstone's rapt, enthusiastic attention. His form was bent forward, his eyes were riveted ; all the intellect and soul of his great nature seemed expressed in his countenance ; and when they had finished he kept saying, "Isn't it wonderful ? I never heard anything like it !" After this they gave us that queer medley, "O them great trials!" with the comical assertion of Baptist, Independent, Presbyterian preferences, and the grand lesson of Christianity *versus* sectarianism. The tender, thrilling words and music of "Oh how I love Jesus!" brought tears to the eyes of the listeners; and when they closed with the "Lord's Prayer," all the company, led by Mr. Gladstone, reverently stood with bowed heads in worship. Then came many hearty farewells, and some time was taken up by our friends obtaining the autographs of Mr. and Mrs. Gladstone and others. Just before leaving the room they sang, "Good-bye, brother, good-bye, sister," which went to every heart. As brothers and sisters, the premier and Mrs. Gladstone, with their guests, bade them one more and last farewell. It was just noon when we passed through the hall, where several persons were waiting on official business to see the premier, who, doubtless, from that time till late at night was anxiously occupied with public affairs, but whose morning was given up to his negro friends with such heartiness and leisure of mind that a stranger might suppose he was, of all present, the one whose time was most his own.

"'London, Eng., July 30th, 1873.'

"To this letter nothing need be added, unless it be the interest manifested by the Right Hon. W. E. Forster, who informed me that his father died while on a visit to the governors of the Southern States in America, for the purpose of persuading them to exert their influence for the abolition of slavery; he also gave me a donation for the Fisk university. Subsequently Mr. Gladstone sent us a very valuable present of books, according to the suggestions contained in his letter.

"The next day we were to take tea with the Rev. C. H. Spurgeon, and give a concert at the Metropolitan Tabernacle. We had looked forward to this event with many fond anticipations. One great desire had animated us from the time we decided to visit England: it was, that we might be welcomed to the Metropolitan Tabernacle by an audience that should completely fill the house. I had early sent word to Mr. Spurgeon by a person who assured me he had his acquaintance and confidence, stating how anxious I was that he should hear the singers. I offered to accompany my friend on his errand, but he thought it quite unnecessary. It was anniversary time, and Mr. Spurgeon was not only unwell, but very much occupied, and I felt it would be cruel to trespass upon his time more than was absolutely necessary, and so nothing further was done than to persuade his personal friends to bring the matter before him in such a way as to secure his attention. The Hon. George H. Stuart from America was in London at this time, and mentioned the singers to Mr. Spurgeon; Mr. Stuart was sure we should find hearty support if we appealed to him. I therefore wrote to Mr. Spurgeon, telling him plainly our wishes, and explaining why we had not pressed ourselves upon his attention with greater perseverance. I found I had not rightly estimated the freedom and forwardness of this great and good man in espousing the cause of Americans. He does not believe in ceremony or middle-men, and is not at all shocked if a person addresses him without introduction. He replied to my letter at once, expressing himself in the following way :—

"'*Nightingale Lane, Clapham, July* 11*th.*

"'My Dear Sir,—

"'You should have come or written to me at once, for I believe in straightforward running, and do not care for influence and persuasion and all that; you and your brother minstrels would have been welcomed as soon as you landed, and shall be welcome now. The only direct application made to me was through Mr. Miller, the hand-bell ringer, and I said yes at once. I wish you had come in to see me; but I greatly respect your kind motive in keeping away, so very few people have any thought of that kind * * * You shall be welcome, and may God bless you.

"'Yours most truly,

"''C. H. Spurgeon.'

"A date was soon fixed for a concert, and Mr. Blackshaw, secretary to the Metropolitan Tabernacle, kindly undertook all the duties of advertising and providing for the sale of tickets. The Sabbath previous to the concert we all went into the Tabernacle for worship, and took the opportunity after service of receiving an introduction to the great preacher. While we were waiting our turn, the people in the room adjoining the one where Mr. Spurgeon received his visitors asked Mr. White for a song. The singers, in their tender, earnest style, sang, 'Oh, brothers, don't stay away, for the Bible says there's room enough.' They had scarcely finished when Mr. Spurgeon summoned them into his presence: he had heard their song, and they had taken his heart; but I will let him tell his story. 'Now I do not know whether you will approve or

## HOSPITALITIES RECEIVED IN LONDON. 85

not,' he said, in the evening service, 'but it seems to me it is the right thing, and I will take the risk. After the morning service I heard the Jubilee Singers sing a piece, "Oh, brothers, don't stay away, for my Lord says there's room enough in the heavens for you." I found tears coming in my eyes, and looking at my deacons, I found theirs very moist too. That song suggested my text and my sermon to-night. Now, as a part of the sermon, I am going to ask them to sing it, for they preach in the singing; and may the Spirit of God send home this word to some to-night—some who may remember their singing if they forget my preaching.' Then followed the singing, with such clearness and power, that all the vast audience of five or six thousand people could hear; some, forgetting themselves, broke out into spontaneous applause with clapping of hands at the close. I have heard it said several persons date their conversion from that evening. Mr. Spurgeon had taken for his text, 'It is done as thou hast commanded, and yet there is room.' He announced the concert for Wednesday, supplementing the notice with the exhortation, 'Oh, brothers, don't stay away,' and as will be seen anon, it sank deep into their hearts.

"The following Wednesday the singers were to meet Mr. Spurgeon at the station, and accompany him to his residence, for recreation and tea, prior to the evening service. I shall ever remember the happy countenance he wore on our arrival, and the pleasant conversation we had with him on the way to his house. There was one remark he made for which I was not prepared; it was that he considered Henry Ward Beecher as the Shakespeare of this century (an idea which I learned later on was not uncommon). Mr. Beecher had done so much for us, we loved him as a father; we adored Mr. Spurgeon as the prince of his profession; and to have the foremost preacher in Europe express such high admiration for 'the foremost man in all the world,' was a tribute of praise fit for the entertainment of even the humblest of Americans. We found that Mr. Spurgeon had selected for himself a beautiful rural retreat at Clapham, and provided a tasteful house, with ample garden grounds. We had no sooner entered than he called our attention to the exploits of an enormous cat which sprang through his arms with the agility of a trained athlete; we found, also, that his grounds were rich in birds and domestic animals, for which he and Mrs. Spurgeon have great fondness. Our stay was very pleasant, and the songs rendered to Mrs. Spurgeon, who is an invalid, gratefully received. Mr. Spurgeon said of them in the evening, 'I am not sufficiently acquainted with music to find fault with the songs I have heard this afternoon, and what is more, I hope I never shall be; but I am sufficiently acquainted with music to be able to say I never so enjoyed music which I have listened to in the way of performance. Our friends seem to sing from the heart; their souls are singing right cheerfully, and this gives a fire to their music that cannot be in it under any other circumstances; they have touched my heart.'

"If any person imagines that Mr. Spurgeon is a genius without study, they have only to visit his library, and see even the books of his own that have been published, numbering some twenty large volumes, to be relieved of their error. Although many of these are books of sermons, yet they were all prepared for the press by him with great labour. For the first time I saw 'John Ploughman's Talk,' and was surprised to find it had already attained a circulation of one hundred and eighty thousand. On inquiring of Mr. Spurgeon if he were able to write this book of Proverbs right on, as one writes a letter, he replied, that it was the product of very great painstaking.

"After tea we were taken in carriages to Mr. Spurgeon's Orphan Asylum at Stockwell. We learned that some devoted lady had given £20,000 to the great preacher, begging him to establish such an institution; while he and his fellow-labourers had raised from other sources a large amount for building. The grounds were ample, the buildings tasteful, and furnished with all essential conveniences, and the system of work very efficient and successful. Every Friday morning Mr. Spurgeon gives his personal attention to the business relating to its management, and there is every prospect that its beneficent work, which is already extensive, will be enlarged from year to year. The deacon, Mr. W. C. Murrell, told me that they kept up the Church collections for it even with the year of our Lord: that is, in the year 1872, they collected £1,872, in the year 1873, £1,873, etc. Other gifts are received through other agencies.

"The Tabernacle was reached by an entrance in the rear, only to find an immense throng of people pressing for admission. An American gentleman reports,— 'The bills announced, "Doors open at seven o'clock"; but long before that, the crowds around the gates were such that they were compelled to open them to avoid a street blockade. At ten minutes past seven there were already four thousand people present. If ever I saw seven thousand they were there last evening. According to the English style, Mr. Spurgeon opened the meeting with a few remarks, and then introduced the singers. It was evident before the singers began that they were to have an enthusiastic reception; the result fully vindicated the confidence of our expectations. The applause was long-continued. Mr. Spurgeon's humour flashed out all the way through; the good nature that *over*flowed so bountifully was so sincere and manifest that nobody could take exception.'

"As for myself, I do not think I ever realized the worth of Jennie Jackson so fully as I did when I saw her stand in Mr. Spurgeon's place, and hold the attention of that vast audience as fixedly as the preacher ever had done, while she sang the gospel of, "You may bury me in the East, you may bury me in the West, but I'll hear the trumpet sound, in that morning." After its conclusion Mr. Spurgeon took occasion to apply a few remarks respecting the absurdity of consecrated burial-grounds. The whole concert was a succession of triumphs. At its close Mr. Spurgeon said,—

"'Now our friends are going to Scotland, and I have told them to come here, and hold their first concert when they return to London. They have come to Great Britain to raise £6,000: they will do it; and if they want £6,000 more, let them come back to this country again, and we will give it to them.'

"The net proceeds of this concert were £214, being by far the largest amount we had received on any one occasion up to that time in England. Thus ended our work for the time in London, and we started, full of hope, on our way to Scotland.

## CHAPTER VI.

#### JOURNEY OF THE JUBILEE SINGERS TO SCOTLAND.

AFTER the doctor and I had completed our visit at Bâle, we departed for Rome, stopping at Milan, Venice, and Florence. A new sensation came over us as we entered the gates of the Eternal City. The spirits of the great and good may never visit the earth perhaps, but there are times when one seems as if surrounded by them. When we walk where Cæsar, and Cicero, and Brutus shook the world by their powers, we feel as though something of these men were left behind. When we entered the catacombs, where, soon after Christ's ascension, His followers hid themselves; when we read the story of the cross in the pictures they portrayed upon the walls more than seventeen hundred years ago, these early martyrs became alive once more; their history spoke when we went to St. Peter's, and stood in the circus of Nero, where the Christians were slain by scores, and gazed upon that wonderful edifice that stands without a rival in the world; when we wandered, meditating, beneath its great dome, and through its magnificent chapels, and around its enormous dimensions, "The blood of the martyrs is the seed of the church," some spirit seemed to say to us. And why is all this? who can fathom God's design in ordaining or permitting it? Artificers, sculptors, painters, warriors, statesmen, orators, poets, historians, and great dignitaries of the church have left their names here: who can comprehend the ultimate reason why the All-wise sent them in such lavish numbers? The doctor and I studied immortal paintings. We went twice to the Pantheon, built before the Saviour's advent; we went to St. Clement's Church, built above another that had been razed to the ground. We wandered through subterranean chapels, and read the pictures on the walls; as the Interpreter led Bunyan's pilgrim, so we seemed to be led from day to day amidst scenes that revealed to us some lesson fresh and new, of the ever-changing and uncertain destinies of nations and men. We were taught as well the enduring influence of suffering with Christ. St. Paul in prison wielded a more reaching influence than Cæsar in the senate chamber, or at the head of his armies. Rome is rich in names and memories, but no names are treasured so lovingly as those of Peter and Paul.

"To be blessed like these men," said the doctor, "requires no expensive diploma, no laurel crown. Peter left his nets and boats—a simple thing, a masterly thing: the one thing for him, because that meant he counted nothing dear of his own, but everything all-important bidden by the Redeemer."

"Great usefulness," said I, "is within the possibility of every man who is ready to expend his energies with such a spirit. Titus conquered Jerusalem and returned to Rome in triumph: the people built an arch which stands by the Coliseum. St. Peter and St. Paul conquered themselves, and the structures bearing their names deck the Protestant world." While we were restoring our souls with such reflections respecting the triumphs of Christianity, we repaired to the Capitoline hill, and, in the gardens of Augustus, took a seat, near a middle-aged lady, who was painting a view of the grounds; and I went on to narrate to the doctor the experiences of the Jubilee Singers on their way to Scotland.

"Before departing for Scotland to make arrangements for the campaign," I said, "I called upon the Earl of Shaftesbury, to ask advice respecting who would be the best man to introduce us to the Scotch people. His Lordship immediately informed me that there was no better man for my counsellor than Mr. John Burns, of the Cunard line of steamers, to whom he gave me a letter of introduction. As I wished to arrange some business by the way, I had secured advice from Dr. Allon concerning work at Hull, Scarborough, Newcastle, and Sunderland. At Hull we decided to give a private concert, and then proceed to Scarborough, where the same plan was to be pursued; at Newcastle and Sunderland we determined to give concerts in halls. On reaching Glasgow I found Mr. Burns as ready to aid us as his noble friend had been to commend him. He invited me to spend the night at Castle Wemyss, where it was decided to give a garden party in August, to which Mr. and Mrs. Burns should invite the leading citizens in the west of Scotland, together with the members of the press, to welcome the Jubilee Singers.

"The preparations for the work in August were for the most part intrusted to the hands of friends. We had been more than three months in London, and hailed with pleasure an opportunity of visiting seaport towns, and whiling away a few days in the summer, with such recreations as these places afforded. The singers were not generally informed respecting the home and fame of Wilberforce at Hull. It was the first of August, and when, entering the town, we passed the fine monument that commemorates this great emancipator, and read the inscription stating that it was erected on the first of August, we felt like those who had come to an anniversary jubilee. Our quarters were at the Cross Keys Hotel, in front of which there is a polished bronze equestrian monument of King William III. The Rev. W. C. Preston had invited about fifteen hundred people from the different churches by cards to the Hope Street Chapel, of which he was pastor, and when the singers entered the pulpit to sing, they were welcomed in such a way as did honour to the memory of their distinguished townsman. Mr. Preston introduced the singers, and they went on with the programme. At the intermission I explained the object of our visit, and urged the people to give with such liberality as would exemplify that the disciples of Christ would sustain a missionary meeting, and work as liberally, if the appeal was made to their consciences, as though an admission were charged. As the people present had been invited from the best of families for the purpose of aiding the mission, I thought it would be a fair test of an experiment we wished to make, to ascertain if we could not raise the money this way, rather than by pursuing the commercial method to which we had been obliged to adhere in America. I made all this as clear as I could, and the collection far exceeded the expectations of the friends present, amounting to £52 12s., which was about one-half what we should have received if admission had been charged. It was almost impossible to bring people to believe that the singers could realize the amount from their concerts which we sought to secure. When Mr. White or I said we ought at least to realize £100 per night, they looked upon us with apparent pity. No benevolent enterprise ever had an agency that could raise money like that; indeed, there was no enterprise whatever in the country, attractive to the better class of people, that afforded its managers any such profits. The grand concerts given throughout the kingdom were more like popular celebrations in America, where distinguished men are secured for the purpose of adding to the enjoyment rather than from expectation of realizing even expenses. I scarcely ever knew a man or society of men who provided a series of concerts in England or Scotland that made money by it; they realized a popular treat for themselves and friends, or advertised their business as music-sellers, and that was all. Low minstrel companies, catering for the vulgar tastes of people, were more likely to do a lucrative business; but their patrons were not to be relied upon for our constituents. Star singers were well paid, and saved money. With such facts before the minds of the better class of people, it is not to be wondered at that they were appalled as we asked £100 for the services of a few children who were recently slaves, and who made no pretensions to being professional singers; with a knowledge of this I was often almost in despair of accomplishing the object of our mission. We had come to the right quarter to revive our courage, however. Before the close of this private concert the Rev. W. M. Statham made a stirring address, insisting (with others) that instead of our going to Scarborough on Monday, we should remain and give a concert, and charge an admission fee. To this we consented, and Hengler's Cirque was fixed upon as the most fitting place for the entertainment. Mr. Dickerson promised to speak on the Sabbath to some children at the Hope Street Chapel; Mr. White and a number of the singers went to the service with him, and found the building crowded to overflowing. Every one present seemed very happy, and the little listeners gave £9 for the library at Fisk University.

"While we were sitting at the window of our room in the hotel during the long evening, witnessing the throngs of people flowing like a tide of life up and down in front of King William's monument, Mr. White felt compassion for the multitude, and proposed, if I would deliver a short address, to sing a few songs to the wandering crowd. We arranged ourselves, therefore, in front of the monument, using the base for a platform. I read a portion of Scripture, songs were sung, prayers were said, while the crowd kept gathering around in ever-increasing numbers. I preached a short discourse, and the singers sang of the love of Jesus to many a soul only accustomed to use His name in blasphemy. While the tears were trickling slowly down the cheeks of the wretched wanderers I felt a new emotion: I saw when a thing good enough to be paid for is bestowed upon poor lost souls it goes straight to the heart we attempt to benefit. If we essay to benefit poor people as dogs are pelted with bones, if we deem anybody and anything good enough for them, our work will fail. Paul might be a fit preacher for the learned Athenians; but Jesus Christ was the all-sufficient one for poor fishermen, for extortionate tax-gatherers, for Magdalens. To restore the spiritually dead, buried in the mire of wretchedness and sin, needs the rarest gifts accompanied with the tenderest heart and the most exalted love for their poor souls. Think thyself never a master, oh mighty one! unless thou art able to gather the poor wretched outcasts in thy embrace, and to robe them in their right minds, and present them to Jesus without 'spot, or wrinkle, or any such thing.'

"On Monday Mr. White accepted an invitation to visit the Humber training ship for boys, and delighted them with attentions and songs, for which the brave fellows raised a little fund and purchased Knight's 'Pictorial Old England,' a valuable book for the Fisk Library; this book was to bear their names and to express their sympathy. In the evening, though the night was rainy, Hengler's Cirque was densely crowded, and the enthusiasm a continued inspiration to the singers. The ardent friends who had aided us so lovingly would not let us go without a promise to return on some future occasion, and as the income of the Monday concert equalled £140, we did not hesitate to give them assurances. At Scarborough we found that the Rev. R. Balgarnie had arranged for our welcome at the South Cliff Congregational Church. His children performed the clerical work of inviting about eleven hundred people by cards, and a very select and appreciative audience honoured us by their attendance. Mr. Balgarnie presided, and though it had been previously arranged that there should be no manifestation of applause, the chairman finally concluded that, seeing the people felt as they did, it would not be right for them to suppress their emotions; so the encores were as free as usual. Many persons were spending their vacation at this 'Queen of watering-places,' and great care had been taken to secure the presence of such as might aid us in the midland counties and the provinces. These people, it was thought, would be pleased to render liberal assistance by their donations. In this Mr. Balgarnie was not disappointed, for although the capacity of his church did not allow of so large an audience as we had found at many places where we had given private concerts, nevertheless the collection was greater than we had ever before received, amounting, after all the money was paid in, to about £90. The singers lodged with Mr. Whittaker, formerly a temperance lecturer of some note, and at that time one of the Town Council. At his house every attention was received. Pleasure parties were formed, invitations accepted, and recreations fitted to refresh us for our future work enjoyed. On Sunday Mr. White had promised to sing to the Sunday School children on the green, and over four thousand persons were present, including a crowd of fishermen and others. Though it poured with rain, the people preferred getting wet through to missing the musical treat.

'Here we made the acquaintance of Mr. Roundtree and his family, members of the Society of Friends, and received from them many hospitalities at the time. A second concert was given in Mr. Balgarnie's church, for the reason that other pastors did not see their way clear to open their places of worship for a service at which an admission fee was to be charged. The concert was quite successful.

"The Rev. H. T. Robjohns, of Newcastle, had entered upon the work of providing for our welcome to his town with the forethought of a general when planning a campaign. He counted the cost, he took in all the bearings of the case, and discovered all the fountains of influence necessary to be opened. He was a popular and accomplished writer, a prize essayist, and knew the thing fitting to be said, and, what was equally fortunate, he had access to the press. He understood the art of nourishing a plant to stimulate a harvest. He did not expect results until he had complied with all the comprehensive conditions for securing them. When we entered the town and learned what had been done, we foresaw the triumph that awaited (I speak advisedly) him. He had sold the house. People who knew scarcely a thing save what he told them had paid their money and pressed together on a rainy night, till the hall was crowded almost to suffocation: no seats could be had for love or money by the time the concert commenced. The Methodists were holding a large annual meeting in Newcastle at the time, yet a very good number of their ministers were at the concert. 'I never trembled so much for a man in England as I did for Mr. Robjohns on that night; if the people he gathered should be disappointed, I shuddered for the consequences to him. No introduction was made. The singers quietly and unannounced rose from their seats, and amidst the hushed stillness gave forth, with the greatest possible precision of time and tenderness of feeling, 'Steal away to Jesus'; this was followed by 'The Lord's Prayer'; and then what a tide of relieved anxiety rolled off the faces of the happy audience! I looked at Mr. Robjohns,—he was saved; he had not wasted himself or misled his friends. As usual the Methodist ministers did justice to their noble religious instincts; to them it was a species of millennial camp-meeting—why should they not be happy? They contribute more liberally for African missions than any other denomination. The Jubilee Singers were like promises for Africa, and promises fulfilled; they were like morning stars ushering in a day of better things.

"Mr. Robjohns had kindly advertised the book containing their history, and the large number we had present were quickly disposed of.

"Large numbers of the Methodist brethren promised us assistance in their several towns, and the Newcastle people insisted upon a return visit from us, on our way from Scotland to the midland counties. At Sunderland, Messrs. Moody and Sankey had been holding revival meetings, and much interest had been awakened in religious circles there, previous to our visit. Mr. Andrew Common and Mr. Campbell very kindly undertook to gather an audience for us at that place, and first brought to my notice the value of patrons. Mr. Common arranged that Mr. J. Candlish, member of Parliament for Sunderland, should take the chair, while the clergymen and ministers of the different denominations were prevailed upon to allow their names to appear on the advertisements, as patrons. This gave a dignity to the movement, besides making an impression that it was an affair of the better class of people. When I made the preliminary arrangements, my friends dared not encourage me to expect £30, and pressed me very hard to issue a threepenny ticket. To this I very seriously demurred. Our lowest American price, as a rule, was twenty-four pence; it was really humiliating to come down to three. I would agree to twelve; but I fear my hopes were regarded as an hallucination. However, under the very efficient management of Mr. Common and Mr. Campbell, the large Victoria Hall was filled, and, it was said, thousands of people went away, who failed to obtain entrance. No such enthusiasm had been awakened in Sunderland for many a day; and the zeal and hopefulness of our benefactors almost put us to the blush as we took our journey to Scotland."

## CHAPTER VII.

#### WELCOME TO SCOTLAND.

AS the doctor and I journeyed from Rome to Naples, we fell into speculations concerning the respective arenas of the world's literature and civilization.

"There may be a different atmospheric influence," said the doctor, "on peninsulas formed either by seas, or deserts, from that existing in the centres of continents. Perhaps magnetisms or electricities come up from the waters, or are generated by the tides, or are borne upon the winds as they journey over the deserts. Early civilization existed in Egypt on a slip of land between the Sahara and the Mediterranean; then came Syrian culture between the Arabian desert and the sea; then Grecian on the peninsula of Greece; then Roman on the Italian peninsula; Spain has a watery boundary, making it as much like a peninsula as its civilization was like those of the countries mentioned; while Great Britain, which has outgrown all these nations in the brilliancy of her illustrious authors, statesmen, and philanthropists, is but an island amidst many waters."

"But how," I asked, "shall we dispose of the question of the failure of these countries to continue producing such men?"

"I do not know," said the doctor, "unless civilization moves in an orbit which ever tends westwards. The Chinese doubtless believe they can boast of the oldest civilization; from them it has ever moved west; Christianity has travelled with it. Peter and Paul went west, the old Romans went west, the Puritans went west, the sons of the Puritans go west, and I sometimes think civilization is bound home to China. Like some life-giving tide, civilization has developed, on its way over peninsulas, great names. Florida and Lower California have the conditions from which we may predict that, according to the foregoing speculations, great men may arise."

As I thought the doctor's speculations rather poetic and of but little worth, I asked him jocosely if he considered there were any atmospheric reasons that influence Mrs. Stowe to repair to Florida every winter to prosecute her work as an author? To which he only replied, "Here we come to the land of Virgil!"

There now broke upon our view the great Neapolitan city. We entered its borders with enthusiasm mingled with awe; we had never before visited a city that kept a volcano, and scarcely knew how to deport ourselves. We took lodgings at the Washington Hotel, and strolled, during the beautiful soft twilight hours, along the borders of the most famous bay in the world. Pompeii, Vesuvius, Herculaneum, and the islands in the bay taught us their lessons, as they had done to thousands of travellers before. There was one spot, however, that fairly captivated the doctor: it was the beautiful eminence where the castle of St. Elmo sits like a crown, overlooking the wealth of historic places on sea and land. To its renowned summit we betook ourselves, and after a delightful review of all our experiences in Naples, I proceeded to narrate the history of the Jubilee Singers' welcome to Scotland.

"As we were to remain in Glasgow for several weeks," I said, "the singers were quartered in lodgings which afforded them comfortable homes. It was not our purpose to attempt a great amount of work before the 1st of October. The wealthier classes were spending the summer months at different watering places, and as it usually rains every day on the west coast, I do not see how they could go amiss in seeking such destinations. People in Scotland repair to the country rather to escape the smoke and dirt than the heat. The thermometer in August is sometimes below freezing-point, while it has been as high as fifty-five Fahrenheit in January; but, notwithstanding, a change is desirable even in the surpassingly healthy cities of Scotland, and during the summer people flock down the Clyde to the many pretty villages that nestle on its banks.

"The next day after our arrival at Glasgow we proceeded about noon to Castle Wemyss, situated on Wemyss Bay, about thirty miles from town. Mr. John Burns' father and mother had kindly prepared dinner for us at their house near the castle, and with other invited guests we experienced the blessedness of Scotch hospitality. Mrs. Burns was ill at the time, but able to listen to the chanting of the 'Lord's Prayer,' which afforded us a grateful opportunity of manifesting our desire to appreciate the kind interest she had taken in our mission. About two o'clock we repaired to Castle Wemyss, where a platform had been erected for the singers under the wall of the house, in front of which the invited guests were seated. Among the distinguished persons present were the Right Hon. the Earl of Shaftesbury and Lady Edith Ashley; the Hon. Mr. and Mrs. Evelyn Ashley; Mr. Dalrymple, M.P., and Mrs. Dalrymple; Sir Peter and Lady Coats; Captain Sullivan, R.N.; the Venerable Archdeacon and Mrs. Prest; Mr. and Mrs. George Burns; Lieut.-Col. Lyster and the officers of the 21st Fusiliers; Captain Dennistoun, R.N.; the Rev. Dr. and Mrs. Hutton; Mr. and Mrs. Elder, of Knock Castle; the Rev. Mr. Kinross, etc., etc. About four hundred people had been invited, among whom were many members of the press. Unfortunately the weather was changeable, and the blasts of wind often stole snatches of the songs away. Indeed, an out-of-door concert by vocalists, unsupported by an orchestra, must ever be hazardous to the reputation of singers, and especially when they depend largely upon the gentle breathing of sounds for producing their best impressions. This party, however, did not come to criticise, but to welcome and aid the singers. They had too much sympathy to hunger for defects, and too generous purposes to remember deficiences. Among other songs they rendered one, by request of the Earl of Shaftesbury, called 'Turn back Pharaoh's Army;' this and the 'John Brown' song altogether enlisted the attention and applause of the entire company.

"As the visitors had been invited by card 'to hear the Jubilee Singers from America,' it was fitting that some statement should be made respecting the object of their mission. Mr. Burns, though abundantly able to make such a statement himself, begged his illustrious friend, who had been his guest for several weeks, to honour his visitors with a few remarks in explanation of the needs of the Fisk University, and the efforts of the Jubilee Singers in its behalf. As I do not remember ever hearing a more concise and comprehensive appeal of its kind, while in Great Britain, than this impromptu address by the Right Hon. Earl of Shaftesbury, I give it in full, not only as a specimen of the genius of this truly lordly man, now, when at the advanced age of seventy-two, but also as setting forth the bounden duty of the English-speaking people to the struggling millions of the African race. His Lordship said,—

"Ladies and Gentlemen, you have heard Mr. Burns state that he has thrown upon me the duty of expressing to you in a few words the reason why the Jubilee Singers are here, and at the same time to tell you who and what they are. I have great pleasure in doing so, because, as I was amongst the earliest of the acquaintances they made on coming to England, I am in some measure capable of telling you the purpose for which they have come here, and the holy mission, for so I may describe it, upon which they have entered. The youngest now present may remember the great war in America, which ended, God be thanked, in the wiping out of the cursed system of slavery from the United States. One of the first results of that great event has been, that the negro race have risen to a sense of their high destiny, and of the station which, by God's blessing, they may hold amongst the civilized races of mankind. Having made a great effort in America for the benefit of their own people, these Jubilee Singers have come here to see whether they can excite a like sympathy, and stir the hearts of the English people to join with them in elevating the negro race to the position to which they are entitled by the laws of God and the great capacities with which he has endowed them. Now, these excellent young people have almost all passed through the ordeal of slavery. Many of them have been sold not once or twice, but thrice, and even oftener. Some of them, too, have been in the dismal swamp, pursued by their masters and by the savage bloodhound; but by God's mercy they escaped, and they now come here to show to you what the negro race are capable of if you will give them those benefits and opportunities which you have yourselves enjoyed. They have undertaken to raise a sum of £14,000 to found a college in Nashville, Tennessee, for the education of coloured people, and they ask our sympathies and co-operation in extending the means and the advantages of that college. They have raised £8,000 in America already, and they expect to raise other £6,000 in Britain. I hold that the mission upon which they have entered is a grand and holy one, and we ought to thank God that people so recently snatched from the degradation and misery of slavery should come here seeking in this way to advance the interests of their fellow-creatures. You have listened to them singing the "Lord's Prayer" with a depth of feeling which I have seldom heard equalled, and in their hymns and songs we have felt the charm of their melody and the exquisite grace and pathos of their style. I believe that from the bottom of their hearts they have prayed as they sang, "Forgive us our trespasses as we forgive them who have trespassed against us." They cherish no feeling of revenge against their past persecutors; all they desire is that the coloured race may be raised to the same level as their white brethren, and that all may walk together in Christian peace and honour and usefulness. I am sure we all rejoice in the freedom which has been given to the slave, nor can we forget that we share the guilt of our brethren in America because of the past existence of that system. We forced that system upon the United States, and, sharing their responsibility, we must also join with them in seeking to assist the emancipated slave. I therefore call upon you, and through you upon all those whom you can influence by your words or your example, to come forward and aid these excellent young people, and to rejoice in fulfilling the words of the prophet—"To undo the heavy burdens, and to let the oppressed go free."' (Applause.)

"During intervals in the programme ices and refreshments were served in a large pavilion erected on the lawn in front of the castle, and the gardens were thrown open as promenades. Before parting, Mr. Burns proposed three cheers for the Jubilee Singers, which were heartily accorded. On the motion of Mr. Dalrymple, M.P., seconded by Sir Peter Coats, a cordial vote of thanks was given to Mr. and Mrs. Burns for their invitation to such an enjoyable entertainment. The company joined with the singers in a verse of the Queen's Anthem, and the students having sung one of their touching parting songs, the company separated.

"Reports of the party filled the columns of the daily papers, and the endorsement of our mission was complete. Before leaving the castle we consulted with Lord Shaftesbury and Mr. Burns as to the best method of introducing the singers to Glasgow and Edinburgh, and the next day I received two letters, one addressed to the Lord Provost of Glasgow, and the other to the Lord Provost of Edinburgh. I was not aware of their contents, but understood from the handwriting that they were sent me by his Lordship. What was my surprise on learning afterwards that they were proposals for the city authorities to vote a welcome to the singers, and to bring them before the public under the auspices of 'the Lord Provost, the magistrates and Town Council of Glasgow and Edinburgh!'

"Many persons at Castle Wemyss assured us of their readiness to aid, and several donations were made for the Jubilee fund. It had been nearly settled by our friends that it would be contrary to the proprieties of the Presbyterians to allow services like ours to be held in their churches, and especially if an admission were charged. I was therefore relieved when the Rev. Mr. Kinross, pastor of the Established Church at Largs, invited us to visit his parish, and not only charge an admission at the door of the church, but to take a collection as well. Mrs. Gamble and party, from Gourock, proposed also that we should give our first concert at the U. P. church in her village, assuring us that her pastor was very much interested in America, and would certainly welcome us. She even agreed to fix the next Wednesday as the time, promising to telegraph at once if she found on her return any obstacle in the way of the proposal. The Rev. David MacRae, her pastor, had travelled through the United States, and had visited many of the schools of the American Missionary Association. He had even devoted a chapter, in his work, entitled 'Americans at Home,' to an account of its missions among the Freedmen. On our arrival, he gave us a cordial reception, and the sight of the American flag, with which he had gracefully decorated the platform prepared for the singers in the church, inspired an enthusiasm not readily forgotten. That flag meant liberty to the poor slaves during the war for their emancipation; when it was seen unfurled in front of the moving battalions, the bondsmen knew emancipation was near; the camp over which it waved was his city of refuge,—the day he entered it he became disenthralled. He had looked to the country of the Queen, hundreds of miles away, as his only land of rest, but the flag of the Union brought to the very door of his cabin a land of liberty. For him it meant a new era, a golden age, a millennial morning. The sight of that flag at Gourock revived fond memories in many a heart, and gave new strength for days to come. About this time it was deemed advisable to appeal to the citizens of Greenock for patronage, as their town afforded the advantages of a watering-place to many of its citizens and friends. As ex-Provost Morton was present at the garden-party at Castle Wemyss, he was fully informed of our purposes, and unhesitatingly gave me letters of introduction to the different ministers in Greenock, and promised, at my request, to take the chair, if a concert were given in the Town Hall. It was therefore arranged to give the concert under the patronage of ex-Provost Morton and a few of the leading clergymen. Letters were sent to all the churches, asking them to give notice of the visit of the singers from their pulpits on the Sabbath, and in many instances the requests were granted. This was our first appearance, in a large town in Scotland, where we were thrown entirely on the public for support, and the occasion was regarded as a test of what we might expect from the Scotch people; we realized also how essential it was for our future work that the meeting should be full and popular. No effort was spared to advertise most thoroughly. And the variety of work done was sufficient to occupy the time of one man for a full week. This labour was not expended in vain in Greenock.

The hall, which accommodates two thousand or more people, was densely crowded, and the sympathy expressed was most encouraging. A few days after it transpired, I received a note from Mr. Morton, proposing to secure the upper balcony of the Town Hall for the accommodation of the lads of the Working Boys' Society, on the occasion of our next visit, which had already been arranged. This proposition was the more grateful to me, as Mr. Morton proposed to pay full price for the admission of the boys, instead of asking me to make concessions. There was another gratifying circumstance in connection with the Greenock concerts. By the law of the town the charges for the hall must be paid at the time of its engagement. I had complied with the rule, but, when the authorities learned the character of our work, through the kindness of Mr. Bailie Campbell, the money for the use of the hall was returned, accompanied with the offer of it for the future. The second concert at Greenock, if possible, was a greater ovation than the first. The chair was taken by Mr. J. J. Grieve, M.P., who gave a fine opening address. During the intermission, Mr. Bailie Campbell said he had in his possession a document which showed that, at the beginning of this century, the Scotch people were very much involved in the trade which America had so recently abandoned, and which

## WELCOME TO SCOTLAND. 115

made it evident that the British people ought to forward the work represented by the Jubilee Singers The paper, a bill of lading, was as follows:—

"'Shipped by the Grace of God, in good order and well-conditioned, by Irving and Fraser, in and upon the good ship called the "Byam," whereof is master. under God, for this present voyage, George Martin, and now riding at anchor in the Respongo; and, by God's Grace, bound for the West Indies. To say— "Two hundred and eight slaves," and to be delivered in the like good order and well-conditioned at the aforesaid port of the West Indies (the danger of the seas, mortality, and insurrection only excepted), under order of their assignees. Freight for the said slaves, paid, vessel belonging to the owners, with primage and average custom.

"'In witness whereof, the master and purser of the said ship have affirmed to three bills of landing, all of this tenor and date, one of which bills being accomplished, the other to stand void. And so God send the good ship to her desired port in safety. Amen.

"'GEORGE MARTIN.

"'Dated at Kessing, 14 May, 1803.'

"'That shows,' continued Bailie Campbell, 'how much we are bound to help them; and I hope when it is known how we in this country sympathize with them, that they will not require to record, as they have had to do, that when they came to some railway stations they were ordered out of the waiting-rooms, and that they were refused accommodation in hotels on account of their colour; and that America would not only have the stigma of the slave trade removed, but would take them by the hand and treat them as fellow-citizens, entitled to every privilege possessed by their white fellows.' A noble aspiration, based upon a generous wish to think kindly of my native land; but on this fourth day of July, 1874, it is heart-sickening to say that, but a few days after the return of the Jubilee Singers to Nashville, two of the most honored ladies of their number were ordered once and again from the ladies' waiting-room at the railway station at Nashville, being threatened with the interference of the police, and also that they were refused a place in the ladies' car, and crowded into a smoking carriage with a dozen chained convicts then journeying to Louisville, to say nothing of being refused refreshment by the way, unless they would repair to a room out of the sight of white travellers while they partook of it; and furthermore, that in the face of these facts the people of the land are, with the exception of an occasional outburst of indignation, sunk in apathy over the whole subject.

"Successful meetings of welcome to the Jubilee

Singers were held about this time at Largs, Dunoon, Killcreggan, and Hellensburgh. At the latter place Mr. Kidston, of Ferniegair, kindly made very acceptable arrangements for the service, issuing cards of invitation to the people of his town, who were abundantly able to aid our work.

"The remarks of Mr. Kidston, during the service, exhibit something of the feeling which exists among Scotch Presbyterians respecting musical entertainments. 'This sacred music,' he said, 'does not, I think, partake of the nature of the oratorio conducted by mere professional singers, which I disapprove of (hear); but on the contrary, solemn words are uttered, I believe, from the heart of every singer. Permit me to say I cannot help thinking God has some purpose to serve with the African race. The *furore* for education at present in South Africa is extraordinary. Having been for some years the representative of Africa in the Free Church Assembly, I have had my attention especially drawn to this circumstance.' With many other English people, Mr. Kidston seems to believe in the vitality of the African race; that they are destined to wear out the other races, and will yet hold a very prominent place among the children of men. At this Hellensburgh meeting the handsome sum of £73 was realized for the singers, and a host of friends secured. Scotland was now unquestionably an open door, and we determined, while waiting the return of the people to the large towns, which would take place about the 1st of October, to pay a brief visit to Ireland."

## CHAPTER VIII.

### IRELAND AND SCOTLAND.

FROM Naples the doctor and I determined to travel direct to Jaffa, in the Holy Land. We therefore took passage in an Austrian Lloyd boat, with several other passengers, bound for the same destination. It seemed as if good fortune had taken upon itself the business of adding to our pleasure. Stromboli favoured us by belching forth fiery eruptions during the first night of the voyage, and the rushing water between Scylla and Charybdis revealed the peril so much dreaded by the ancients. We thought much of the shipwreck of Paul, and of his faith, as we glided over the waters of his memorable voyage. In four days we came in sight of Alexandria, and twenty-four hours later steamed up to the coast of Jaffa. There were neither whales like Jonah's, nor visions like Peter's to welcome us, but camels, donkeys, and Arabs in abundance. It was early in the forenoon when we landed, and accordingly we determined to proceed towards Jerusalem the same day. The doctor and I procured horses for the journey, and riding out of the town through extensive groves of orange and lemon trees, that were laden with the richest of fruits, we soon came in sight of the hills of Judea, where we proposed to tarry for the night. The next day we made our way to Jerusalem, and doubtless, like most travellers, were much disappointed to find it an unattractive city, containing about eighteen thousand inhabitants. On our way we had seen a hill decked with olive trees, which our dragoman told us lay over against Bethlehem. As the distance from Jerusalem to this town was only six miles, the doctor and I proposed to walk over to it the next day. The thought of the vast throng of worthies who had traversed it before, added an interest to the journey that can only be felt. I did not indulge in conversation; it was a time for reflection. Great tides of emotion kept surging over me; I knew I never should think and feel as I did then, again, and I wished that the impressions might be stereotyped on my soul. When we came to the top of the hill that overlooked the Church of the Nativity, we turned from the road, to a quiet enclosure to meditate. Did the star come hovering over this place with its beam of promise? Did angels, with countenances like lightning, and with robes of the purest white, come sweetly over these hills with words and songs, to awake a slumbering world to life and joys unending? "Behold, I bring you good tidings of great joy, which shall be unto all people." That angel song shall never cease until every human soul has heard it. "Shall be unto all people." How the prophecy seems still to be reverberating! Where was it the "glory shone around"? we instinctively asked: in what pasture or glen were the shepherds waiting? How did the wise men, with their gold, frankincense, and myrrh, move about these grounds,—seeking their way beneath the gleam of the star, till it stood over the place where the young child lay? Bethlehem was the city of David: was he allowed to accompany the herald angels on this night that preceded eternal day? Rachel's tomb is near the town: was Jacob allowed to come and attend that memorable birth, near where his beloved partner died? Indeed, so many inquiries came flooding upon us, that we sat in silence hour after hour, to be refreshed with the histories and faith that were our inheritance.

"It is good for us to be here," said the doctor. "Let us turn to our work in hand; a break in our reveries will only make them the sweeter when we return to them."

I went on, therefore—reluctantly, I fear—to give him an account of the work done in Ireland and Scotland by the Jubilee Singers.

"When we left London," I said, "we were so well introduced, that the services of two clergymen were no longer needful, and the Rev. Mr. Powell returned to New York, and entered upon labours in my collecting field. Meanwhile Mr. Stoughton, of the firm of

Hodder and Stoughton, had arranged with Mr. J. Hamilton Halley, one of their clerks, to assist me for a definite period. As my assistant's grandfather, the Rev. R. Halley, D.D., was well known throughout the kingdom, and as his father, the Rev. R. Halley, M.A., had a few years ago been President of Doveton College in India, he was well fitted for securing the co-operation of a large number of good people who had learned to honour the family to which he belonged, while the vicissitudes of his life had not only prepared his mind, but also his heart, for such exigences as were incident to the Jubilee Singers' work.

"During the time Prof. White and the Jubilee Singers were fulfilling engagements on the Clyde I proceeded to Ireland, to arrange for meetings at Belfast and Londonderry, leaving Mr. Halley in charge of work to be done at Perth, Dundee, and Aberdeen. Mr. John Burns, whose fleet of Cunard steamers surpasses the German navy in number and tonnage, had given me letters to his agents in Ireland, and on my arrival at Belfast I was welcomed at once by Mr. McCullum. The Hon. George H. Stuart, of America, was born in this part of the country, and is held in great esteem by the people, who remembered that during the great famine he was the first to send a vessel from America with supplies. Mr. Stuart had spoken of the singers to many of his Irish friends, and I was authorized to use his name *ad libitum* to further my work.

The people, however, were little informed about the Jubilee Singers, and the task of arousing an interest was difficult at first. Mr. Burns they knew, and Mr. Stuart they knew, and it was mainly because of this that we were enabled to secure our patronage. Mr. McCullum gave up the day to me, and, taking a jolting car, we pursued our way from office to office, securing the names of one magistrate and another, under whose auspices we assayed to bring the Jubilee Singers before the public.

"The kindness of the President (the Rev. P. Shuldham Henry, D.D.) of Queen's College was exceedingly gratifying. He welcomed our enterprise with genuine Irish enthusiasm, and his name and counsel made it possible to complete such arrangements as were essential to success. Placing his name at the head of a list of five magistrates and several justices of the peace, we advertised the concert for Ulster Hall.

"'The audience,' said a Belfast paper, 'was one of the largest and most fashionable we have seen in the hall for a considerable time; and they had the advantage of enjoying a troupe of real negro choralists, whose appearance was as widely different from the Christy's as the character of their programme, and who, without the aid of cornermen, a skedaddle breakdown, a burlesque *prima donna*, or a plantation walk-round, succeeded in delighting the enthusiastic listeners.' The solo of Miss Minnie Tate was especially praised. 'She was greeted with a well-deserved encore, and responded by giving a plaintive air, which wandered away into a wild strain of music, in which the other members of the company took parts, the chorus being one of the sweetest, perhaps, given throughout the entire evening.'

"There were several circumstances connected with this visit to Ireland which seemed providential. One was that the Jubilee Singers were in a sense a reward to Irish people, for their interest in the African race. Some time previously Miss Hamilton, of Belfast, had given £1,000 to the Freedmen's Mission Aid Society of London, under whose auspices the singers were labouring. To her the singers were an illustration of the work her money had promoted. Friends in Belfast had also contributed to support Miss Mary Kildare, a missionary from Ireland, who had rendered much useful service to the American Missionary Association, among the Freedmen in Virginia and North Carolina. Her friends rejoiced in their labours when the Jubilee Singers sang. Perhaps the most gratifying circumstance was one published in the *Northern Whig* by the Rev. James M'Kee, a missionary who had laboured in India. He writes,—

"'Sir,—It will, I am sure, be interesting to your readers to know that the pioneer of those noble institutes for the education of the Freedmen in Tennessee was a county Down man, named Joseph G. M'Kee, of Lochaghry, brought up under the ministry of the Rev.

R. Moorhead. While a boy he emigrated to America. The following notice from the *Nashville Daily Bulletin* affords a brief review of his experiences:—It says, "Ten years ago the Rev. J. G. M'Kee was a proscript in this city, houseless, homeless, like his Master, having not whereon to lay his head. After the labours of the day, spent in feeding the hungry, clothing the naked, and visiting those who were sick and in prison, he wrapped himself in his blanket, and slept during the night on the stone steps of the capitol. And what had this man done, thus to become a pariah in a Christian city, from whom the good should turn as from a leper, and against whom the door of every hotel and boarding-house was closed, until at last he was taken in by a friendly coloured man, whose daughter, as if by a just recompense of Providence, has since sung before the *élite* of America and the Queen and nobility of England? This, and nothing more. Protected against the mob by Federal bayonets, he had founded a school, open to the child of the Freedmen as well as to the child of the Freeborn. In accordance with the gospel preached, he put in practice the truth, that God 'is no respecter of persons.' Burned out with his fiery zeal, overtaxed with his labour of head and heart, he laid down and died, a martyr to his cause, having already seen something of its triumphs. But as the blood of the martyr is the seed of the church, so this noble life was not sacrificed in vain; for see the fruits of his labour and sacrifice, and of those of others devoted to the interests of the downtrodden. It must be a source of great satisfaction to them, the most of whom still live to see with their own eyes what they now see." From the seeds then sown,' continues the Rev. Mr. M'Kee, 'sprang up the Baptist Theological Institute, the Central Tennessee College, and the Fisk University.'

"It will be seen, therefore, that our Irish friends justly claimed a goodly part in those triumphs which were incidentally celebrated by the Jubilee band; and that they illustrated how God gratifies His people by allowing many of them to realize how they are of assistance in labours of love. What is more gratifying than to be a yoke-fellow, a joint-heir, a judge upon the throne with the King of kings? Even this world gives us many glorious foretastes. We gave several concerts at Belfast, and received much assistance from the Rev. William Johnson, Moderator of the General Assembly of the Presbyterian Church, and also from the Rev. Wallace M'Mullen, of the Methodist Church, who met the students at Newcastle-on-Tyne, and subsequently not only made them known through the papers and pulpits of Ireland, but also assisted me in arranging for the details of the work in Belfast. From Belfast the students went to Port Rush, from which they visited the Giant's Causeway, securing specimens from it for Fisk University; and from thence they proceeded to Londonderry. I had previously arranged for the 'Service of Song' in this town to be given in the large Presbyterian Church. The pastors of this historic place were desirous to aid the Freedmen, and full of zeal for missions, but had never been called upon to weigh the expediency of such methods as were pursued by the Jubilee Singers. Mr. M'Niel, one of the elders, entered into our project with great enthusiasm; while the Methodists and the Congregationalists were active and confident. Meetings of the trustees of the Presbyterian Society were called, and after we had promised to omit from our programme the 'Three Fishers,' the 'John Brown' song, and indeed any others that might be styled secular, the use of the edifice was granted. The mayor promised to occupy the chair, and the concert was largely advertised. I realized that there was a feeling of uncertainty in the town as to the high character of the services of the singers, and consequently experienced great relief in reading in one of the Londonderry papers the following communication from one of the magistrates of the town :—

"'THE JUBILEE SINGERS IN BELFAST.
*(To the Editor of the " Sentinel.")*
"'DEAR SIR,—
"'I had the pleasure of hearing this wonderful troupe last evening in the Ulster Hall, and I can assure your readers that they have a rich treat before them on Friday night. From the

notices in the papers I expected a great deal; but I was not prepared for such strange, thrilling, delightful music, rendered with such ease and pathos, as I heard last night. The singers return to Belfast next Tuesday, at the earnest request of many influential people.

"'Your obedient servant,

"'ROBERT M'VICKER.'

"Mr. M'Vicker's well-known character and extended influence acted like a charm upon his townspeople, and on Friday evening the house was well filled. On the Sabbath Mr. Rutling addressed a meeting in the Congregational Church, while others of the company attended the Sabbath-school services at the Presbyterian Church, where Jennie Jackson spoke a few words to the children and sang. In the evening I preached to the people. During our stay we were intensely interested in the history of the great conflict that once was waged in this town: we wandered over the walls and stood by the gates where, nearly two hundred years before, Protestantism engaged in a tremendous struggle, and achieved a glorious and lasting victory. The city was small, but full of courage. At one time twelve hundred papists, led by the Earl of Antrim, were ordered to march against it, by the authority of King James II., when thirteen young apprentices, most of whom were of Scotch descent, flew to the guard-room, seized the keys of the city, rushed to the ferry gate, closed it in the face of the King's officers, and let down the portcullis; an older citizen warned the officers to go, and at the cry of 'Bring a great gun!' the intruders retreated to the other side of the river.

"Subsequently the eyes of the Protestant world were turned to this spot, as for one hundred and five days the people of Derry endured almost every form of suffering, during the siege carried on by the King. Horseflesh and tallow formed the staple of food. A little fish, when caught, could not be purchased with money; dogs fattened with the blood of the slain were luxuries, while even rats were eagerly sought and devoured.

"It is said that a fat man thought it prudent to conceal himself, as he suffered so constantly from such a devouring gaze of people in the streets as suggested cannibalism. After more than half of their number had perished, relief was received from England, and the army of King James abandoned the siege. At this time the tide turned strongly in favour of Protestantism throughout England; and Londonderry will ever be remembered as a battle ground where sufferings were experienced that accomplished wonders for the overthrow of Roman Catholicism and the reign of the Stuarts.

"The Jubilee Singers were esteemed by the citizens of Derry as another company of young people turning back a tide of ignorance, cruelty, and prejudice. When the second concert took place they were very well understood. The senior pastor of the church occupied the chair, and though with his elders he had not favoured applause, or the rendering of some of the songs usually on the programme, yet under the circumstances he felt that the suppression of feelings was a violation of the normal expression of religious emotions, and therefore undesirable. He also wished the students to sing the 'John Brown' song. Mr. White, however, assured him that it was impossible, stating withal that they had been granted the use of the church upon the express condition that this song should not be sung. The authorities were therefore consulted, the restrictions removed, and the song sung, much to the joy of all those liberty-loving people of the north of Ireland. By this time I had word from the Lord Provost of Glasgow that he wished to see me, and I accordingly arranged for a return to Scotland. On my arrival I found that the Lord Provost, the magistrates, and the Town Council of Glasgow, a city of five hundred thousand inhabitants, had voted to welcome the singers under the patronage of the city authorities, and to introduce us at the City Hall in the best possible way. I can scarcely comprehend this act even at this day. A King, a Queen, or the President of the United States might be welcomed by the rulers of a great and rich city on behalf of its people, but for a formal welcome to be bestowed upon a few children who were sometime chattels, or indeed treated as cattle in my native land, is almost past belief. It was really so, however, thanks to the Right Hon. Earl of Shaftesbury, who had asked so much for us. The Lord Provost of Glasgow is the highest functionary in the city, and this made it all the more pleasing to have his goodness shown towards us. 'This is a cause,' he said to me, 'in which I believe, and I am willing to do all I can for it.'

"Mr. J. Muir Wood, the proprietor of a large music warehouse in Glasgow, had been visited by Mr. Burns and Lord Shaftesbury, and asked to render us advice and assistance. By his aid, and that of Mr. George Gallie and Mr. MacCallum, we were able to provide for the proper performance of everything essential for the convenience of the *élite* of the city at the evening concert. Although the singers had received many honours, they had never experienced one precisely like this, and were as ambitious as ever to acquit themselves in a manner creditable to their patrons. The City Hall was filled, and the platform was occupied by the Lord Provost, magistrates, and clergymen of the city. His lordship made a pleasing address of welcome. The singing was received with a kindly interest throughout the evening, and especial notice was made of the solo rendered by Minnie Tate. Toward the close of the entertainment I expressed our gratitude to the city; in reply to which the Lord Provost responded, 'That he was sure he expressed the feelings of every one present when he said that he never attended a more delightful meeting; he could not help feeling that the exquisite music they had heard would be long remembered. It was marked by a tenderness of expression, and, above all, a solemnity, which made them feel they would be all the better men and women for having been there that evening. Mr. Pike had spoken of thanks being due to the magistrates for their countenance; but he thought they ought rather to give thanks to the Jubilee Singers, and he proposed that they should give them a cordial vote of thanks.' The Rev. Mr. Somerville also addressed the meeting, expressing the wish that Glasgow might make up the amount needed for the Fisk University; while the Rev. Dr. Wallace proposed a vote of thanks to the Lord Provost for presiding. Subsequently Sabbath services were held in the churches represented by these clergymen, and at a meeting of the Foundry Boys' Society, when liberal donations were given for our enterprise. Mr. Halley meanwhile had arranged for the appearance of the singers in the north of Scotland, and cordial welcome was accorded to them at Perth and at Dundee, the chief magistrates of these towns occupying the chair on the evenings of the concerts. At Aberdeen they were able to accomplish a variety of services. Mr. Hector, Secretary of the Sunday School Union, arranged for a Union Sunday School meeting on the Sabbath. Here, as we had found elsewhere, there was manifest some hesitation as to the use of the Jubilee Songs in the church, the Scotch people being largely confined to psalm singing; they sometimes indulge, however, in certain paraphrases. I endeavoured, therefore, to prepare the way, by stating that the hymn commencing, 'O how I love Jesus!' was in every way proper, and that the audience might be asked to join in it, then if the singers were left to sing it alone, no one could complain. This arrangement prepared the way, and the vast crowd of grown-up people, who had been admitted into the capacious galleries of the church, seemed to approve the method, and wept like children as the sweet mellow notes of that hymn of hymns was breathed forth, with the utmost affection and tenderness, by the singers. I am persuaded it would have been almost deemed a sacrilege for any other voice to have mingled in the delightful harmony. The Rev. Dr. Brown was sitting by, watching with the deepest emotion the phases of joy which glowed upon the countenances of many listeners. Addresses were delivered and hymns sung by the children, till I ventured to suggest that it would be hardly right to allow so many little ones to return to their homes without having heard a single slave song, and asked if it would not be acceptable if the singers would render, 'O children, don't stay away, for Jesus says there's room enough, room enough in the heavens for you.' Dr. Brown and the other clergymen present were altogether agreeable, and the meeting on the whole seemed as satisfactory to the people as the appreciation and contributions were to the students. On Monday evening a service was given in the Music Hall, which was well attended, and on Wednesday a private concert to distinguished persons from the country, in the drawing-room at Dr. Dyce Brown's residence. Among those present were the Countess of Kintore, Lady Madeleine Keith Falconer, and the Hon. John Keith Falconer, from Haddo House; Lady Katherine Gordon and party; and Sir William Seton, Bart., of Pitmedden, etc., etc. 'It is needless,' says the *Aberdeen Free Press*, ' to say the performance was in all respects most interesting and successful. The visit of these strangers from another land will long be remembered. The progress they have made in a comparatively short time under the able direction of Mr. White, the Treasurer of Fisk University, who accompanies them, is nothing less than wonderful. The materials he has had to deal with in most of these songs are quite out of the usual course of musical subjects. Mr. White may well be congratulated on what he has been able to accomplish.'

"A second public concert was given in the Music Hall, at which the Lord Provost occupied the chair. 'The audience filled every corner of the hall, and at the close of the meeting the Lord Provost, in a single sentence, bore testimony to the enjoyment they had all experienced from the musical abilities of the Jubilee Singers.' During the summer the Hon.

George H. Stuart had advised me to call upon Mr. Thomas Nelson, of the firm of T. Nelson and Sons, in Edinburgh, and consult with him respecting our appearance in that justly-celebrated city. He was out of town when I called; but his brother at once afforded me assistance, and took me to Mr. Thomas Knox's office, where we canvassed the subject in a most thorough manner. Mr. Knox had been one of the magistrates of the city, and exerted a great influence, especially in affairs pertaining to the temperance question. He had learned about us before my arrival, and was able to suggest the best method of procedure. Through him I secured the services of Mr. John Grey, who attended to most of the details of the seven concerts we gave at different times in that city. Mr. Cowan, the Lord Provost, wrote me a kind note in reply to the letter he had received from the Right Hon. Earl of Shaftesbury, and promised his co-operation in bringing the singers before the public. Subsequently I was informed that the magistrates and Town Council had voted us a welcome, and we were accordingly advertised to appear under their patronage. There was a trifling outburst of loyalty when the vote was passed by the city authorities that was not displeasing. In advertising the advent of the singers I had followed the chronological order of events, and stated that they had appeared before his Excellency President Grant at the White House and before Her Majesty the Queen. One of the city fathers thought it was scarcely courteous to their sovereign to mention the name of our President first; but I make no doubt a notion of our good intentions on the whole quite atoned for this seeming indiscretion, as I have the impression that the vote of welcome was quite unanimous. On our arrival in Edinburgh, the Lord Provost invited me to his office, and proposed that the singers should meet him with a few friends at a dinner party, on a given occasion. We had often been out to tea, and sometimes to breakfast, but had no experience of a fashionable dinner-party in town. Prof. White and the singers accepted his invitation, therefore, with much gratitude. The introductory concert took place in the Music Hall, with the Lord Provost in the chair, and, like all the subsequent meetings, was successful in every way. A very large number of Christian gentleman and ladies were present on all occasions, and their interest showed how much people of refinement enjoy natural outgrowths of pious emotions. The attentions bestowed upon the singers were more than of a transitory character, while presents of books and money from one and another testified to their high appreciation of our mission. As the incidents of the concerts were much as usual, I will only mention at present the hospitalities received at the residence of the Lord

Provost, and as the Rev. Dr. Hanna, son-in-law and biographer of Dr. Chalmers, in his letter to Mr. Thomas Nelson, gives a good account of the impression made by the students when at the house of the Lord Provost, nothing can be more fitting in this place than his words.

"'*Edinburgh, Oct. 31st*, 1873.

"My Dear Sir,—

"It was a very happy thought of our Lord Provost to invite the Jubilee Singers to dinner. I have been present at civic banquets given by former Lord Provosts, and have looked round with pride and pleasure on companies composed of some of our most eminent fellow-citizens, or distinguished strangers who happened at the time to be in Edinburgh; but I never looked with such pride and pleasure on any of them as on that assembled in the house of our present Lord Provost on the evening of the 16th of this month.

"' When dinner was announced, I was asked to take down Mrs. Cowan, and had already made a movement to do so, when somehow it occurred simultaneously to both of us that it would be more becoming in me to select one of our coloured guests. Acting at once upon this prompting, I found myself seated at table betwixt two of the female band of singers, and more intelligent or better-mannered companions at table no one could desire. After such an education as they have received at Fisk University, I was prepared for the intelligence; but I own that I was not prepared for the quiet, unassuming, cultured manner.

"'When after dinner, the health of the Jubilee Singers was given, one of their own number (Mr. Dickerson,) in responding, said: "Ten years ago I was a slave: to-day I am not only enjoying all the privileges of a free man, but find myself sitting at such a table as this, surrounded by such kind friends,—ten years ago I was subject to the auction-block and the lash: to-day there is no auction-block and no lash in all the United States," I own to a thrill of gratitude and joy such as has seldom passed through my heart; and when, in words and manner the most appropriate, he proceeded to say that "he trusted that they would prove worthy of the deep sympathy and interest that their friends had taken in their enterprise, and that the negro race might yet be a people that no nation would be ashamed to own," I am sure that it was the common and deep feeling of all around that too much interest, too much sympathy in such a cause as that which he and his companions represented, could not be shown, nor could too bright a hope be cherished as to the destiny of the negro race, if only the means of Christian education with sufficient promptness and in sufficient measure be supplied.

"'I am, ever truly yours,

"'To Mr. T. Nelson.'  "'WILLIAM HANNA.

"About this time we had completed arrangements for concerts at Paisley, Kilmarnock, and Ayr, the birthplace of Robert Burns. Mr. Stewart at Kilmarnock had supported one of the missionary teachers at Fisk University, and was therefore able to look upon the Jubilee Singers in some measure as the product of his benefactions. In his town a most gracious welcome was bestowed upon Mr. White and the students. At Paisley Sir Peter Coats and Messrs Clarke, Hutton, and Hodge, with the members of the Tonic Sol-fa Union, and many others, were assiduous in their care to render all needful co-operation. The first-named gentleman had taken a very hearty interest in all our movements in Scotland, and I had frequent occasion to consult him respecting our best interests. Some men are born noblemen, and some, through the grace of God, make themselves noblemen. Sir Peter is one of the latter class. His father established a small business in Paisley as a manufacturer of thread, and attained some little prosperity. There were several sons, and Sir Peter's mother wished him to enter the ministry; after a time, however, he judged it his duty to follow his father's occupation, and the great popularity Coats' thread has attained attests to his ability as a manufacturer, while the good he has accomplished by his services and wealth remind us that there are powers outside the pulpit that are very potent. I know of no man in any country who has made a more indelible impression on my mind, or better illustrated how one may be 'instant in season,' and what many might excuse themselves in calling 'out of season,' in serving the Lord. Sir Peter has a country house near Ayr, on the banks of the 'Bonnie Doon,' bearing the poetic name of Auchendrane. I twice had occasion to visit this beautiful spot at his invitation, and to share his company one time on the way. He met no man, woman, or child, without imparting a blessing. The blessing was in his heart, and flowed out spontaneously, at the sight of each individual. At one time it was for a poor fellow who opened the door of his cab, at another for a clergyman whose wife was dangerously ill, next for a girl who received toll at a gate, to whom he gave such kindly counsel that the memory of it has blazed in my soul like a divine light. His servants and even domestic animals regarded him with an affection that a king might envy. When a man is a baronet, it is not certain whether he be good or bad, as that title may come to him by the accident of his birth; but when a person is created a knight, so uniformly is it now the rule to confer titles for merit, the presumption is that he is a man of great personal worth. He has his title by appointment; it is a reward of merit; but you may meet his Grace the Duke, or his Lordship, and be quite uncertain as to his quality.

"It was Sir Peter's plan for us to take tea with the

town clerk of Paisley, and give a 'Service of Song' in a church near in the evening, and he devoted himself to the completion of proper arrangements.

"On taking the chair at the concert he delivered an excellent address, stating the object of the singers, and saying that on two previous occasions he had listened to their songs, and been charmed. He also quoted remarks he had heard from Lord Shaftesbury, and thus prepared the way for a generous reception of the singers. The success of this concert justified our making arrangements for a second, which was given in a larger church. On this occasion the singers were invited to the establishment of Messrs. Whitehill and Co., when each of the young lady singers was presented with a Paisley shawl as a memento of their visit to the town, while the young men received specimens of local manufacture. In addition to these favours, Sir Peter secured the use of a church for us in Ayr, and introduced me to the Provost of the town, who invited me to come, with my wife, and remain at his house during the stay of the singers. This land of Burns, and, I might almost say, of Sir William Wallace, abounds with charms for Americans, and all of us were anxious that the singers should enjoy all the suggestions the haunts of the poet afforded. The next day after the concert, therefore, Sir Peter conveyed the company first to the birthplace of the poet, and then to Alloway's old Haunted Kirk, and the famous bridge that spans the Doon, over which Tam O'Shanter's mare escaped from the witch. Every foot of ground in this locality is famous with memories, and, like other travellers, we refreshed our minds with the rustic poet's songs, and gathered relics for ourselves and friends. A few persons had been invited to meet us at Auchendrane, where dinner was provided. Lady Coats and her daughters entertained the students with many attractions, afforded by the rare taste of Sir Peter at his country home, while Prof. White and myself were invited to tell the friends who were present of our future hopes respecting the Fisk University. We said we hoped by the aid of the singers to provide a building. After that was finished others must endow professorships, and provide money for the support of the students; and we begged them, if they approved of the part we had undertaken, to devise means so that our labours might not be in vain. Before our departure Sir Peter presented each of the singers with a beautiful memento of the land of Burns, and, with much consideration, added to the gift presents for Mr. White, Mr. Halley, and myself.

"He also spoke words of encouragement to some of the students, which cheered them through the remaining labours of the campaign.

"During all these days there were various comments made respecting the quality of the services rendered by the students. Musicians did not agree. Every one approved of the enterprise, and heartily sympathised with the young people; but some could not understand the reason for enjoying so simple, natural, and unpretending a performance as they gave. This led to kindly criticism, which aroused the generous heart of Mr. Colin Brown, Ewing Lecturer on Music, Andersonian University, Glasgow. He wrote a series of papers, that were published somewhat extensively, and through them many persons realized why they had pleasure in the singers, notwithstanding preconceived notions of what alone was truly excellent. Mr. Brown wrote,—

"'What is the charm which these Jubilee Singers have brought with them across the Atlantic, which acts so powerfully upon all classes of our people? Their music is beautifully simple. So also were the Swedish melodies of Jenny Lind. So also are all the gems of national melody—" Ar-hyd-y-nos," " Robin Adair," " Tutti tutti," " Katherine Ogie," and " Gramachree "; but surely such music is not beyond criticism: and when Wilson sung his Scottish songs, or Jenny Lind her Swedish melodies, surely their singing was not the less worthy of notice because they laid aside all professionalism, and sang with the most perfect simplicity and naturalness the songs of their homes. So also with the Jubilee Singers: their songs are the songs of their people, for they had no homes. The melodies, in all their simplicity, are touching, effective, and characteristic. Why is it that at one time they stir up their audience to enthusiasm, and then melt them into tears? Whence is the secret of this wonderful power of their music — like Sappho's of old? Surely it is within the critic's province to examine and to tell. * * We forget that the highest triumph of art is to be natural. The singing of these strangers is so natural that it does not at once strike us how much of true art is in it, and how careful and discriminating has been the training bestowed upon them by their accomplished instructor and leader, who, though retiring from public notice, deserves great praise. He has shown us how to call forth the true genius and power of natural song, and made us feel how "one touch of nature makes the world kin." Would that some one would arise to do equal justice to the songs of our native land!'"

## CHAPTER IX.

### REVIVAL WORK.

AFTER the doctor and I had visited the Church of the Nativity and Solomon's Pools we returned to Jerusalem for the night. Here we found that at sunset all shops were closed, and no places either for amusement or instruction opened. We also observed the absence of strong drinks. The Moslems use coffee and tobacco, but it is against the rules of their religion to drink wine or even beer. They have a very high regard for chastity, yet polygamy is allowed and is not considered sinful. They believe in bestowing gifts upon the poor, and I was informed that one reason why the Turkish government made no provision for its paupers was because begging developed charity.

It had been our purpose from the first to visit Jericho, the Jordan, and the Dead Sea, and we accordingly took up our march for those places through the wilderness of Judea.

"I never realized before," said the doctor, "that so many of the memorable incidents recorded in Scripture took place on so limited a tract of country. From the days of Abraham to the advent of our Lord, most of the events precious to memory occurred in a space over which a man might travel in a day. Walk from Hebron to the Jordan, looking to the right and left, and over the river, and you see the land of Abraham and Lot, of Jacob, the Land of Promise, where stood the cities of the plain, the land of Samuel and Saul, of Elijah and Elisha, of David and the rulers of Judah, the land of John the Baptist and of our Lord. From the time the Queen of Sheba visited it till this day people from all nations come here as to the spot where God and the angels most frequently came. Nowhere on earth have there been so many revelations, and voices, with angel visits, and I cannot but feel that somehow we are near to the celestial gates."

While he was thus discoursing we came in sight of the Dead Sea, and after tedious hours of travel reached its shiny waters. Never lake or ocean presented to my sight such fascinating brilliancy; but clearness and beauty may exist with coldness, bitterness, and death, as is illustrated by other examples than this typical lake. From it we passed on to the Jordan, and from thence to Jericho, where we spent the night. The next day we visited the fountain of Elisha, which was by him miraculously healed, and then we assayed to climb the rocky steeps of Mount Quarrantania, where tradition has it that our Lord was led up to be tempted of the devil. Here, near the site of a chapel, we sat down to view the wonderful scenes of sacred story. The Dead Sea reminded us of the justice of God, the rolling Jordan of His miraculous mercy; there, by its banks, the children of Israel encamped till the waters were divided by miracle; there both Elijah and Elisha parted the waters and passed over; there Naaman washed and was clean; there John baptized; and there "One mightier" came. Before our eyes lay the Promised Land, Gilgal, and Jericho. Marvellous events had occurred in those places from the days of Rahab to those of John. What especially occupied our thoughts, however, was, that we might be on the identical spot where the Saviour endured His temptation.

"When Satan showed our Lord the cities of the plain," said the doctor, "I think he pointed to them as specimens, and promised Him a world of cities as beautiful and rich."

"But," I added, "Jesus had seen another specimen city on the plain below; it was a city of refuge to those who fled from the wrath to come, and its gateway was by repentance and baptism, and its business faith, hope, and charity. John the Baptist had gathered the people for the founding of it. The Holy Ghost came when the King thereof was baptized into it, and the voice from the cloud proclaimed this King *The Lawgiver* from henceforth. This new kingdom was to fill the whole earth. Would Jesus abandon it for the best of Satan's promises? That was the question then, and it was not unlike the one that has grappled with the children of this kingdom since that day."

"Every church," said the doctor, "is a township in this kingdom, and every revival of religion a sign of the King's especial presence, and of His purpose to go on conquering and to conquer till Satan's kingdom is overthrown."

This remark led us into a long consideration of the place of revivals of religion in the history of the church, from the days of the Baptist down through the centuries till the present; when the doctor asked me to tell him of the great awakening in connection with the labours of Messrs. Moody and Sankey, which had been participated in, to some extent, by the Jubilee Singers. I accordingly went on to say,—

"Messrs Moody and Sankey entered upon their work in Great Britain at York, on the first of July, 1873. It had been Mr. Moody's desire for a long while to make the 'Service of Song' a prominent feature in his revival work, and he had been persistent until his method was approved. When the gospel is sung into the heart it seems to make for itself an abode. The tender word of invitation repeats itself like an echo. It lodges and is willingly entertained. This is especially true when the song is rendered by a loving disciple of Christ like Mr. Sankey. From him go forth words to convince, to allure, and to save. I have often heard it remarked by Prof. White," I went on to say, "that no person could sing sacred melodies in the best possible way without high moral qualities of mind and heart. The incense must come from a burning altar; there must be a heart-felt rapture; there must be an intelligence competent to lay hold of the deep things of God, so that the song may come freighted with love and sympathy and knowledge. And more, the song must be sung for Jesus, not for applause or pay. Mr. Sankey has the moral, intellectual, and heart qualities needful for one who would sing the Gospel; to this is added a rich, clear, well-cultivated tenor voice. Some correspondent has well said of him that 'he sings and plays with pathos, touching tenderness, and a spirit full of love for souls. His renderings of " Almost persuaded," " Jesus of Nazareth passeth by," "Oh, prodigal, come home, come home," are very effectual in bringing sinners to Christ.' When I first heard these brethren, and saw them surrounded by eminent ministers of the Gospel, I instinctively asked why men, who could not boast of superior position or learning, should outstrip the properly trained ministers of the cross in revival work, while further reflection led me to believe that it was largely attributable to the fact that they were filled with unusual faith, and that they selected from the Scriptures those doctrines and precepts especially fitted to arouse the conscience, and that these were pressed upon the sinner with an earnestness and persistency that would be almost irresistible if presented by any preacher whatsoever. Mr. Moody breaks up the fallow ground, and Mr. Sankey's music is like an angel's song at the pearly gates, to invite the troubled sinner in from the perils of a perishing world. These men believe in immediate action; now, to-day, is their time. When Mr. Moody wished a large sum of money in Chicago for a benevolent purpose, the friend to whom he applied answered that it was a subject over which he must needs pray. 'That is so,' said Mr. Moody; 'let us fall on our knees and ask the Lord about it.' When the Catholic priest told him he admired his zeal, but wished he was in the true church, 'You must pray for me,' said Mr. Moody. 'I will do so,' was the reply. 'But,' said Mr. Moody, 'let us kneel down and pray about it now'; which was accordingly done, much to the gratification of the priest, who loved him from that hour. Mr. Moody preaches for the immediate conversion of sinners. After successful services at York, he went on to Sunderland, and laboured prior to the visit of the Jubilee Singers. His work helped to prepare the way for them. The effect of the preaching and singing at this place was well illustrated, not only by the large number of conversions, but by touching incidents. One day Mr. Moody had been preaching on the return of the prodigal son, and at the close of the sermon had asked Mr. Sankey to sing, 'O prodigal, come home, come home!' A young man who had been in a backslidden state, came up the aisle to his father and mother, who were godly people; he first put his arm round his father's neck and kissed him, and asked his forgiveness with many tears; then kissing his mother, he asked her forgiveness also. The audience was so overcome that they were obliged to retire to the vestry. Such scenes were so manifestly the work of the Spirit, that the large towns in the vicinity began to long for the services of these American brethren. About the first of November, while they were labouring at Newcastle-on-Tyne, the Jubilee Singers visited that town. The Rev. H. T. Robjohns, who had arranged for their visit, took an early opportunity of commending them to Messrs. Moody and Sankey, and these brethren asked the students to sing one of their slave songs at a revival meeting. I was not present, but Mr. Moody told me afterwards that when they sang, 'Steal away to Jesus,' they stole his heart and led him at once to appreciate the power of their music for good. On November 12th the people of Newcastle and vicinity held a great religious convention, which lasted seven hours, during which time many persons did not remove from their pews. The meeting was one of the most solemn and delightful. The Jubilee Singers were present, and one of the ministers of the town wrote of them,—

"'Their songs are so intense in their spirituality that strong men bowed in tears, not only before the might of music, but before the sovereignty of religion, so that they helped on the revival. They have been present daily at our noonday prayer-meetings, where Prof. White and one or two of the gentlemen have spoken and prayed, and all have sung. One day last week the effect of their singing was magical. For the Wednesday evening the telegraph had been worked to get them an engagement. God in His Providence said no; there was no town that had at once a hall big enough and power to organize a concert with sufficient celerity. So the singers had to remain in Newcastle, their temporary home, and went to a special service in perhaps the biggest church in the town. Messrs Moody and Sankey were there, and there the only one of the party not in Christ found the Saviour. The following morning one soul whispered it to another, till nearly all Christians in the town knew it. The Thursday noon prayer-meeting was largely attended. The latter part of the meeting was open and free as usual. The Jubilee Singers had been specially prayed for. A moment's pause, and then went up in sweet, low notes a chorus as of angels. No one could tell where the singers were,— on the floor, in the gallery, or in the air. The crowd was close, and the singers, wherever they were, were sitting. Every soul was thrilled, for this was the song they sang,—

> "There are angels hovering round
> To carry the tidings home."

The notes are before us as we write, simple enough, the words too, but one should hear the Jubilees sing them. It was like a snatch of angelic song heard from the upper air—as a band of celestials passed swiftly on an errand of mercy. Your correspondent can never forget it. Nor are these all our obligations to our beloved friends. They have gone in and out the churches, Sunday-schools, and mission-rooms singing for Jesus; and in one instance at least went into a sick room, two of them, to sing to a dear friend of ours. Such services to souls and Christ have opened wide the people's hearts, and the Jubilees have just walked straight in, to be there enshrined for evermore.'

"While the events mentioned by this writer were in progress, Miss Susan Gilbert, one of the missionaries of the American Missionary Association, who accompanied the singers, was taken very ill, as the result of overwork; and the sympathy awakened in her behalf, not only among the students, but the townspeople, intensified the religious feelings of all acquainted with the circumstance. From this time to the end of the campaign our minds were never relieved from serious anxieties respecting the lives of one and another of the party who came with us from America. These things led to increased prayerfulness and thought respecting the preparation of souls for eternity.

"It is impossible to follow the influences for good the labours of the singers at Newcastle diffused. They were much appreciated by Messrs. Moody and Sankey, as was sufficiently shown by the latter, who presided at their last concert at this time in that town, in place of Mr. Moody, who had consented, but unfortunately could not be present. From Newcastle the singers proceeded to the midland counties, while Moody and Sankey went on to Carlisle and thence to Edinburgh, where Prof. White, with the students, joined them about Christmas. At this place a 'great awakening' was destined to work almost a revolution in the religious life of the people. It is a notable fact that the great and good men who rule in the churches and institutions of learning in that intelligent city entered into the movement with a profound reverential devotion to the cause of Christ. Noonday prayer-meetings, lectures on the Bible in the afternoon, preaching services in the evening, with inquiry-meetings, were the order of the day. Indeed, on several occasions as many as six meetings were held in one day, at which the singers were present and sang. Like his Master, Mr. Moody is especially thoughtful for the salvation of the poor, and often plans meetings for their benefit. One of this character took place in the Corn Exchange, at which about 5,000 persons were present. The Jubilee Singers sang, and Mr. Moody and others conducted the services, making them lively and full of interest, as is well illustrated by the following incidents which were told during the evening. Col. Davidson told of a young lady who was so much concerned about her soul one night that she arose and wrote in her diary that she would close with Christ's offer of salvation in one year; but this did not satisfy her conscience, and so she changed the date, and wrote that she would give herself to God at the end of a month. After retiring, however, she was so troubled in mind she rose again and entered in her diary that she would close with Christ's offer that day week. In the morning when she arose the impression was gone. She went to a ball that night, caught cold, and continued ill and in delirium till the middle of the following week, when, reason returning, she exclaimed, 'I am a week too late—I am lost,' and passed away. After this recital Mr. Sankey sang, 'Too late, too late, ye cannot enter now.' Mr. Moody began his address by telling an incident in the history of Rowland Hill and Lady Erskine. Her ladyship was driving past a crowd of people to whom Mr. Hill was preaching. She asked who the preacher was, and on being informed told her coachman to drive nearer. Rowland Hill, seeing her approach, said there was a soul there for sale. 'Who will bid,' he said, 'for Lady Erskine's soul? There was Satan's offer: he would give pleasure, honour, position, and in fact the whole world; there was also the offer of our Lord Jesus Christ, who would give pardon, peace, joy, rest, and at last heaven and glory.' He then asked Lady Erskine which of these gifts she would accept? Ordering her footman to open the carriage door, she pressed her way through the crowd to where the preacher was, and said, 'Lord Jesus, I give my soul to Thee; accept of it.' Mr. Moody went on to urge his hearers to follow Lady Erskine's example, and that of others who had recently given themselves to the Lord. His remarks were followed by Mr. Sankey's singing, 'Jesus of Nazareth passeth by.' Perhaps, however, the meeting longest to be remembered took place on one Sabbath evening. Eight thousand of the working people were invited by card to meet Mr. Moody in the Corn Exchange, and between six and seven thousand were present, all standing crowded together. The singers rendered slave songs, while Mr. Moody conducted the services in the usual way. The most perfect order was observed, and the deepest interest manifested in the proceedings. After its close a meeting for inquirers was held (for those who at the meeting at the Corn Exchange had felt their need of salvation) in the Free Assembly Hall, and about seven hundred were present; and when the question was put, if there were any anxious about their souls, the whole body rose in answer. The interest shown was such as had not been seen by ministers labouring long with the people, while Mr. Moody expressed himself as more impressed by it than he had been by anything he had seen before. Soon after this the engagements of the singers took them from Edinburgh, while Messrs. Moody and Sankey went on with their labours in Scotland for months, working great changes in the religious life of the people in the larger towns, where frequently audiences of fifteen thousand and upwards were gathered at meetings held in the open air."

"But," inquired the doctor, "did the singers feel a continued interest in such work after their separation from these evangelists?"

"Prof. White and some of the number did," I replied. "Mr. Dickerson conducted many revival meetings, that were followed with much interest, and Mr. White and the singers held services on the Sabbath in several towns, with good results. At Blackburn, when about to take the train for Manchester, a young lady told Miss Sheppard that one or two persons who were at the Sunday meeting had indulged hope in the Lord Jesus, while many expressions from Christian friends warrant us in saying that every meeting held by the singers in Great Britain, whether it be concert, missionary, or revival meeting, was as great a blessing to souls as a preaching service would have been.

Preaching, praying, and singing are all combined in many of the slave songs, and the memory of them as sung by the Jubilee Singers will doubtless encourage many hearts to offer the prayer and sacrifice needful, that the kingdoms promoted by revivals of religion may fill the dark land from which the black man came, while the memory of the students themselves will give confidence in the Fisk University, which has been a school of revivals since the day it was founded."

"I hope it may be so," said the doctor, "for a missionary college full of the revival spirit is absolutely essential to the great work of training labourers to penetrate Africa with Gospel tidings."

"To be sure," I said; "and the fact that after Moody and Sankey's labours at Glasgow seventy-one men offered themselves as candidates for foreign missionaries, where before it was difficult to find any, illustrates how much we have to hope in great awakenings, not only for the people among whom they occur, but for the whole world."

When so much had been said, we departed from the mountain, and went on our way to Jerusalem.

## CHAPTER X.

### WORK IN THE MIDLAND COUNTIES.

THE doctor and myself were in the Holy Land at the time of the Greek Easter, and witnessed many interesting celebrations. The people on these occasions array themselves in holiday attire, and indulge in relaxation from ordinary labours. The women go from the city in companies by themselves, and sit in groups about the hill sides and amidst the tombs. I remember, one day, passing out of Jerusalem through St. Stephen's gate, and down the hill near Mary's tomb, and the garden of Gethsemane, amidst crowds of these Moslem women. As I beheld them on the steps towards the city, robed from the crown of their head with flowing white garments, I could not but be reminded of the visions of the Apocalypse. As the doctor and I toiled up the slopes of Olivet, we fell into conversation respecting the vast numbers of the disciples of Mahomet. Why do these people value Jerusalem so highly? Why have they built here the finest mosque in the world? Why do they journey over this mountain to a spot they venerate as Moses' tomb ? Why do they guard sacred places, memorable for the sufferings of our Lord ?

"There is something to study respecting this religious sect," I said, "that may be useful to us. They believe that Mahomet will appear in Jerusalem at the general judgment of mankind, but that Christ will be their Judge. There are 170,000,000 Mahometans in the world, who have the Koran in the Arabic. Many of them can read it, and that tells them the New Testament is true. During the past few years Dr. Von Dyke has translated the Bible into this language, and many Moslems are reading and admiring the Word of God. So far as Mahometanism extends, so far it is hoped the Arabic Bible may be read, and that as the Holy Spirit breathes upon its teaching the millions of Islam may come to a knowledge of the truth."

"Yes," said the doctor, "and the fact that they are prayerful, and familiar with Old Testament history on the one hand, and have no habits of gaming or intemperance on the other, encourages us to believe that at the "eventime," when it shall be light, these people may be illuminated and come out from a partial knowledge of God to the fulness of the riches of Christ. God taught His people to understand the Law of Moses first, then He gave them the law of Christ, and He may lead the Mahometan from his prophet to our 'Prophet, Priest, and King.'

By this time we had reached the summit of Olivet,

## WORK IN THE MIDLAND COUNTIES. 161

where it was understood I should give an account of work done by the Jubilee Singers in the midland counties.

"Although more money was made by work done here than elsewhere," I said, "yet there was a sameness as to the methods of securing it that would not bear repetition. Prominent amongst the events of interest were those that brought to us many presents in money and books. The Rev. Mr. Robjohns had arranged a meeting at Darlington, where many Quakers reside, —and these, we knew, had great sympathy with us. The first appearance of the singers at this town was at a private concert. Prof. White made a statement of the necessities of the institution, and asked for money to furnish rooms in the Jubilee Hall, announcing that £10 would be required for each room. Liberal donations were given, and a report of the proceedings published in the Darlington papers. At Durham Mr. Hall achieved astonishing success for the singers. The Rev. J. Hunter had provided for our welcome at York, and obtained not only the patronage of the Church-people and Nonconformists, but had secured Mr. Alderman Leeman, M.P., to occupy the chair. This gentleman had read the Darlington papers, and on being introduced to me gave £10 for a room to be called by his name. The fact was made public by way of suggestion, and was followed with good results at York and elsewhere. At this time I was stationed at

Leeds, and had arranged, by the assistance of the Rev. Dr. Campbell and others, a private concert for Bradford. Mr. White and several of the leading clergymen, with myself, addressed the meeting, and, assisted by Mr. F. Priestman, about £150 were secured, which was the largest contribution of money we had ever received, either in Great Britain or America, as the result of a single meeting. Mr. Edward West, a member of the Society of Friends, presided at our gatherings. Sir Titus Salt, who was unable to be present, sent a donation of £25. The Rev. Eustace Conder, M.A., chairman of the Congregational Union, gave me a cordial welcome to Leeds, commending our enterprise to Mr. Edward Baines, M P., who kindly gave his patronage, and addressed the people at one of our concerts. Mr. Conder also introduced us to the deacons of his church, who gave every assistance in securing patronage and in advertising our work. The constant kindness of Dr. Scattergood and his wife, members of that church, was among our most grateful experiences in this country. The Rev. A. Wood, of the Free Methodist Church, had met us at Scarborough and prepared the way for the singers in many of the churches; while Mr. Archibald Ramsden, the proprietor of a large music warehouse, interested himself exceedingly in enabling us to have a reception worthy of our cause, and of his town. The first concert, which took place in the Town Hall, afforded greater financial results than any we had given before in the kingdom. Subsequently the mayor of the town honoured us by presiding at one of our meetings, and the Sabbath-school children gave a liberal donation for the furnishing of a room in Jubilee Hall, to be named after Mr. Conder's Church. About this time the ministers of Huddersfield, in concert with Mr. Councillor Denham, provided for us a grateful welcome; while the Rev. Mr. Dale, of Halifax, arranged for a concert in that town. Here we met John Crossley, Esq., M.P., whose name is widely known. The mayor presided at the concert, which was crowded to overflowing. In thanking him and the people for the grand ovation we had received, I ventured to say that two things were coupled in my mind: one was the fact that we were in the town justly celebrated for its carpets, and the other that we should need carpets before long for the Jubilee Hall. At the close of the meeting, while bidding Mr. Crossley good-night, he promised the carpets.

"We had never forgotten our promise made in the summer to return to Hull, and accordingly I informed Messrs. Preston and Holdich we would visit that town in December. Mr. Halley went on and completed arrangements for two concerts, which were given, much to the satisfaction of all who were interested. At the first of these Prof. White gave an account of the success attained since our last visit, and also suggested that, as many persons were contributing towards the furnishing of Jubilee Hall, it had occurred to him what a good thing it would be for the students in the University if they could have before them continually an object-lesson, in the shape of some memorial of Wilberforce; it would be a good remembrancer of their visit to the native town of this great emancipator, if a bust or picture of him could be placed in the library of Fisk University. Subsequently a subscription was raised, mainly through the great exertions of Mrs. Preston and Miss Holdich, who themselves collected most of the money, and a fine painting of this great philanthropist was procured and presented to the Jubilee Singers. On the Sabbath there was a large gathering of Sunday-schools in the artillery barracks, and about three thousand children were present. The assembly was presided over by the Rev. Dr. Mackay, author of 'Grace and Truth,' who exerted a healthful influence upon the singers at the time, and followed them with affection and labours during their stay in England. He also gave the University a set of plates of his justly celebrated book.

"Mr. W. W. Shaw, of Rochdale, a young man of uncommon enterprise, had advertised our coming to his town, and secured all the needful assistance required for success. Rochdale, which is the home of the Right Hon. John Bright, can boast of the finest Town Hall we have seen of its size. This was filled with a superior class of people to meet us, and the generous pride they took in advancing our interests made a great impression on my mind. Though Mr. Bright was not present, his family was well represented, and subscribed £10 for a room to bear his name in the Fisk University. Some time afterwards he wrote the following, by way of introducing us to Birmingham:—

"'*Rochdale, December 23rd, 1873.*

"'DEAR SIR,—

"'I have heard the Jubilee Singers, and they have been in this town, where they met with great success. I believe they intend to pay us another visit. I hope Birmingham will receive them kindly; for your great city showed a wise and hearty sympathy with the United States during the great struggle which delivered the slaves from their bondage. The mission of these singers is one deserving of all support, and I feel very certain it will find a multitude of friends in Birmingham.

"'I am, truly yours,

"'JOHN BRIGHT.'

"As most of Mr. Bright's letters go the round of the papers, what he says in commendation is ever destined to exert great influence. It was so in the case of this letter. There was no end to the benefit we received through it, from the day of its date till the close of our campaign.

"At Bolton Mr. Smithies and others entered into our plans with perseverance and devotion. As the result, an audience completely filling the Town Hall awaited us on our arrival, the mayor occupying the chair

With pleasure I learned that the Rev. Chas. G. Finney, the evangelist, who had long been connected with Oberlin College in Ohio, once preached to the people of this town during a great awakening. Mr. J. P. Barlow, who had given us his patronage, aided him largely in his work. I ventured, therefore, to suggest that as Mr. Finney was largely identified with the education of the officers and missionaries of the American Missionary Association, it might be a gratification to him if rooms were named after Mr. Barlow and himself in the new Jubilee Hall. The suggestion was thought a good one, and Mr. Barlow gave us £50 for five rooms. About this time Prof. White, with the singers, made a brief visit—to complete engagements promoted mainly by Mr. Halley—to Dumfries, Dunfermline, Falkirk, Hawick, and elsewhere in Scotland, where they were received with great kindness. Mr. William Kerr, of Dumfries, an eminent nurseryman and florist, made arrangements for a successful concert; and to the kindness shown the singers at the time, he added the honour of bestowing the names of some of the party on different species of flowers which he had developed in his conservatories. He also presented a large number of seeds of rare plants to Miss Sheppard for the Fisk University grounds.

"While these engagements in Scotland were being fulfilled, I established myself at Manchester to complete our plans for the midland counties. The Hon. George H. Stuart, of America, had mentioned our mission to Mr. Henry Hargreaves, of this town. Soon after my arrival he introduced me to Mr. Richard Johnson, the apostle of what is called 'Ragged-school work' in this country, but which is termed 'Mission or Sunday-school work' in America. This brother is a master-workman; he understands the meaning of 'principles and pressure.' When he knows he is right, he goes ahead; and thousands of poor boys, and poor men and women too, know the magic of his voice, and the bounty of his purse and heart. He is not one of your 'goodish men.' He puts his foot upon the rock; he knows the value of a financial basis. He will make money for you; but knows enough to provide for himself also, and in this sets a healthy example to young men.

"As he had had experience in arranging for lectures and large religious gatherings, I looked upon him from the first as a most valuable assistant, and the love I bear him is among the things that will never die. Mr. Johnson and Mr. William Armitage secured for me the best of patronage, with the mayor of Manchester in the chair for the first night, and the mayor of Salford for the second. Our plan of work was this: First, ten thousand circulars of one kind were distributed by reliable men at the best residences in Manchester and in the surrounding towns. These simply announced the concerts. Ten thousand other circulars, with names of patrons, etc., were prepared for the pews of churches. Letters were written to leading pastors, who were solicited to allow the circulars to be placed in pews; then a man was sent with them to make sure the work was done. Newspaper articles were prepared by our friends and published in the papers, and large photographs of the singers placed in windows, while big bills were posted about the city. Ministers were also interested to give notice from their pulpits of the object of our mission and the date of our coming. This variety of work was needful in all the places where the singers were to appear, and the delays in getting patronage and securing other essential arrangements were often exceedingly embarrassing. Help could be obtained; but men able to achieve success in our work were busy achieving success for themselves in other ways; while men who were disengaged, were not competent to grasp the business and push it to a successful issue. Master-workmen are scarcely ever unemployed. To this amount of work, which must be done under the eye of some one, was added the business of answering applications for the singers which flowed in from every quarter. For one, not acquainted with the different towns, it was impossible to decide where to go without much investigation; while it was equally important to see that you did not place yourself under the wrong influences. Many offers of assistance had to be declined because it was needful for success that we should be heralded by persons of great influence. All these things combined brought such incessant labour and anxiety, that before the Manchester concerts occurred I found myself overcome with nervous exhaustion, and obliged to retire from the centre of business, while Mr. Halley and my wife brought me occasionally a statement of the progress of the work. This condition of affairs threw a very large amount of labour upon Mr. Halley and Mr. Johnson; but Providence favoured our movements, and the four Manchester concerts in the Free Trade Large Hall were pre-eminently successful, the proceeds amounting to over £1,200 from sale of tickets, and the profits from the sale of the 'History of the Campaign for $20,000' for a single night equalled £40, or more than $200. The Rev. A. J. Bray arranged a Missionary meeting at the Cavendish Street Chapel, at which a liberal contribution was made, while contributions from other services swelled the amount of our funds. In connection with the Manchester concerts I had arranged for three at Liverpool, to take place in the Philharmonic Hall. Mr. David Stuart, a brother of George H. Stuart, of America, took an early interest in our visit, and introduced me to men of influence, while Mr. William Crosfield kindly secured the patronage of the different members of Parliament and other distinguished personages. Mr. Henry Sudlow, secretary of the Philharmonic Society, undertook the management of the sale of tickets, while the Rev. Hugh Stowell Brown promised me he would take the chair at the first concert. The charges for the Philharmonic Hall being very high, the price of the best seats was fixed at four shillings. The method of advertising was nearly the same as that pursued at Manchester, and the receipts of the concerts were very encouraging, the amount taken at the first from sale of tickets being £325. The *Daily Albion* said of it, "They had not sung a dozen notes when the audience knew that it was not to be disappointed. The marvellous quality of the voices, that strange sympathetic power, which is not the possession of an individual but the dower of a race,—which has often been described, but can only be known by hearing it,—at once arrested attention. On the whole the first concert of the Jubilee Minstrels must be pronounced a great treat and a genuine success.' The singers were lodged at the North-Western Hotel, where only a charge of 8s. per diem each was made. Here, as elsewhere in the United Kingdom, great favour was shown us by the hotel proprietors. In America we had experienced trouble enough from this class of public benefactors; but no more magnanimous or liberal treatment was bestowed on the Jubilee Singers in this country than that received from their hands. They seemed to pride

## Work in the Midland Counties. 171

themselves in showing kindness, and in reducing their prices to the very lowest in order to aid us. Indeed, we were sometimes fearful lest we should offend because unable to patronize all the first-class hotels that were desirous to give us a welcome. On the way from Liverpool to Manchester a concert was given at St. Helens, where Mr. Fenwick Allen had made arrangements, which proved very successful. The mayor, who was unable to preside, sent me £5 for the cause. Mr. Butcher, of Bury, undertook all arrangements for a concert in his town, which proved a financial success. Before the meeting, the singers met a large number of influential ladies and gentlemen at tea, and passed a very pleasant hour. At Doncaster the Rev. G. R. Bettis, with a number of influential Quakers and Methodists, helped us; and, though they had only a week's notice, the Exchange, holding about fourteen or fifteen hundred, was completely filled. They also organized Sunday meetings, which were addressed by Messrs. Dickerson and Halley, and at which collections were made. The concerts and meetings given in January yielded us a gross income of \$19,000. So much business needed to be created and completed in about a month's time, while the amounts received were mostly in sums of from 1s. to 3s."

"But," asked the doctor, "was not the reputation of the singers so great as to render so much advertising superfluous?"

"We scarcely ever had the greatest possible amount of money in the house," I went on to say; "for though a moderate-sized hall could be filled at low prices, with only the ordinary methods of advertising used by persons giving public entertainments, yet in order to sell a large number of reserved seat tickets at 3s. each, a great amount of pressure was needed, while the space that might well be occupied by such people was hardly ever filled. These facts were constantly before us, and had their influence in all our methods of work. By the 1st of February I had so far recovered as to venture a journey to the South of England to advise respecting work in London, Brighton, and elsewhere. During these days Prof. White was fully occupied, preparing programmes, giving concerts, and replying to invitations to breakfast, dinner, and tea, to asylums, schools, and churches,—in a word, invitations of every description from those interested in the Jubilee Singers. As we asked the public for their benefactions, the public, after rendering assistance, wished to bestow, and also to receive, many favours. And as Prof. White accompanied the singers at concerts, and lodged with them at hotels, very much of the pressure of this kind of work fell upon him. To this must be added the business of caring for the various wants of eleven young people, who had been brought into very prominent notice without passing through the long course

## WORK IN THE MIDLAND COUNTIES. 173

usually pursued by persons who achieve distinction. These varied cares were as much as one man could possibly endure.

"At Brighton I called upon the Rev. Mr. Albrighton, who had met us at Newcastle-on-Tyne, and who at my request had engaged the large Dome of the Pavilion for two concerts. When he saw how very ill I was, he kindly took me to Mr. Beves, a prominent Methodist brother, and asked him if he could not aid me. Accordingly I explained to these brethren what I wished done, upon which they assumed the responsibility of securing patronage and advertising the concerts, while I repaired to lodgings in the hope that a few days of absolute quiet would restore my strength. I had hardly become settled for rest before receiving a telegram stating that Mr. Halley, after his laborious efforts in arranging concerts at Stockport, Macclesfield, and elsewhere, was entirely overcome by work, and that the doctor would not allow him to give the least attention to business. Meanwhile, Mr. White's family at Glasgow were ill, and in a disturbed state of mind, resulting in part from the fact that their servant-girl had been taken ill with small-pox. Miss Gilbert was still unable to render service, and was staying with Mrs. White. All these circumstances were exceedingly trying, and especially to Mr. White, who was obliged to remain with the singers or abandon the work that had been arranged for February. One concert was given at Wakefield, under arrangements made by the Rev. Mr. Whitamore, and two at Sheffield, where Mr. Samuel Doncaster, and Dr. Webster, the American consul, had been assiduous in arousing this famous old town to a genuine enthusiasm for our cause. A large new hall had been completed about the time of our visit, and the audience that welcomed the singers was at once attractive and profitable. There were very heavy fogs during these days, and the effect of them, especially upon Mr. White, whose lungs were not strong, was serious. Soon after learning of Mr. Halley's illness I went on to Birmingham and stationed myself there to provide for work in that vicinity. At Derby I met Mr. White and the singers, who were fulfilling an appointment arranged by Mr. A. Butterworth. Here very great interest in our work was manifested, and large donations given in response to Mr. Dickerson's appeal. As the gross income of our concerts at this time averaged nearly £200 per night, and as we were sure it was 'now or never' with us, Prof. White and I decided that, notwithstanding the illness of his family, Mr. Halley, Miss Gilbert, and myself, it was plainly our duty to go forward with the work. I am sure no one can ever estimate the terrible sacrifice this resolve was to him, considering the condition of his wife's health at the time. As for myself, I dared not undergo the excitement of a concert, while the pressure of business, that could not be postponed, demanded all my strength. Mr. White was called upon either to sacrifice his work, with the great income that was being received for missionary purposes, or his desire to be present with his family in their sore trials; for Christ and His Gospel he chose to deny himself. After he had fulfilled engagements at Wolverhampton, promoted by Mr. William Bird, and at Coventry, where Mr. Thomas Beamish had rendered me much assistance, he went on with the singers to Norwich on Saturday, to fulfil engagements which Mr. J. J. Jarrold had made for the following week. While he was at that town and burdened with the complicated duties imposed by the sickness of all his associates, he received intelligence that impressed him with the conviction that his wife was more seriously ill than he had supposed. He immediately left for Glasgow and I came to Norwich to assume his responsibilities as far as I could. On reaching his family, Mr. White discovered that his wife, who was suffering from typhoid fever, had sunk very rapidly and was probably past recovery. No endeavors of the ablest physicians were of any avail, and in less than two days after his arrival Mrs. Laura Cravath White passed away and entered upon her reward. She had been a missionary of the American Missionary Association at the Fisk University, where, by her rare good sense and kindly disposition, she had exerted great influence. Her health had been impaired for several years, and at times she suffered acutely both in body and mind. A knowledge of these things added to the anxiety continually experienced by Mr. White in all his travels with the singers. Her death to him was a terrible blow, and one from which a person of his exquisitely delicate sensibilities could not easily recover; while all who knew her felt that they had lost a strong support, a wise counsellor, and a loving friend. The Rev. Mr. Somerville, Messrs. Moody and Sankey, Mr. John Burns, and Mr. Colin Brown, with others, extended every office of labour, sympathy, and affection to Mr. White in the day of his great sorrow. Mr. James Stuart, of Manchester, tendered him the hospitalities of his home for his motherless children; and God seemed to speak through his little boy, who greatly surprised him at family prayers by reciting, 'Let not your heart be troubled; ye believe in God.' Mr. White's bereavement was followed by loss of sleep and appetite, which so reduced his strength as to render it impossible for him to take a very active part during the remainder of the campaign, while at one time he was utterly prostrated by hemorrhage of the lungs, which led his friends for many days nearly to despair of his life.

"In the condition of affairs at the time of Mrs. White's death our thoughts of the demands of business were in a measure obscured by our troubles. Mr. Halley and Miss Gilbert were still sick, and Mr.

# WORK IN THE MIDLAND COUNTIES. 177

White was away; but the work must go on, as the routes had been laid out and the appointments made. I had availed myself for some weeks of the services of Mr. Matthew Lawson, of Leeds, while my wife, who, like Mrs. White, had come to the country without any relation to the work, or expense to the mission, had volunteered what help she was able to render. On reaching Norwich, to fill Mr. White's place, I found many circumstances favourable for success, and was encouraged by the kind attentions of numerous friends, who contributed both time and money to our cause. At this place Mr. Dickerson received liberal donations for the library fund. Our next appointment was at Ipswich, famous with memories of Clarkson, whose life had been devoted to the abolition of slavery. Mr. Rees, after I had informed him of Mr. Halley's sickness, gathered the people for our concert in the best possible way. The mayor (Dr. Chevallier) occupied the chair. During the interval between the parts I stated the business the American Missionary Association had in hand, and gave an account of what was being done for the furnishing of Jubilee Hall, after which Mr. Lewis Goss gave Mr. Watkins £10 for a room, and £10 more was the next day given by representatives of Needham Market Temperance Society; while Mr. J. D. Piper presented us with copies of the portrait of Mr. Thomas Clarkson for the Fisk University. The Rev. Dr. Matthew Robertson, of Cambridge, had invited us to his town, and had taken upon himself the oversight of all the details needful for giving us a grand welcome to this old city of colleges. The chair was taken at the concert by Neville Goodman, Esq., M.A., and an overflowing audience was very generous in its sympathy and applause. Money was given for a room on condition that it should bear the name of Dr. Robertson, who had contributed so largely in furnishing his townspeople with the pleasure of hearing and aiding the Jubilee Singers. No better report can be given of the impression made than is found in his own words when he said, 'Their songs vary greatly. At one time it is the wail of a heart that is breaking; at another, it is a crash like the trumpet of doom; and again it is the sweet lingering cadence breathed by a glorified soul. But whatsoever be the theme of the strain, it is always intensely real, and hence electric in its power. The musician and the philosopher are alike baffled in the attempt to give a scientific explanation of the spell they throw upon an audience. But the spell is there; and I am persuaded that its secret lies among the deep springs of the heart of man, which are too seldom touched."

"Mr. Thomas Cook, the excursionist, had taken a great interest in all the movements of the singers from the time of their arrival, and had often counselled me respecting our methods of work. I asked him, therefore, to assume the labour preparatory for our introduction at Leicester, where his family reside. As he was from home most of the time, the greater part of the management fell upon his wife and daughter, who, in company with Miss Deacon, provided for our reception. I never met with more kindly or efficient workers. Mr. Ellis, the President of the Midland Railway, invited me to his house and confirmed his expression of sympathy by giving me £20 for our mission. The Rev Mr. Ryder, of Nottingham, very kindly secured for us patronage, and Mr. Henry Farmer, the proprietor of a music warehouse, advertised our work. The singers made their stay at the George Hotel, and received from the hands of the landlady such attentions and encouragement as won for herself the love of the entire party. Mr. Alderman Howitts, the mayor of Nottingham, occupied the chair. The house was densely crowded in every part, and especial mention was made in the papers of the solo sung by Miss Mabel Lewis. The success was beyond all reasonable expectations, and fully justified the reputation of the town for its patronage of good enterprises. The Rev. C. Clements kindly invited Thomas Rutling to return on the following Sabbath for the purpose of addressing a missionary meeting in the interest of the fund for furnishing rooms, and the invitation was accepted and a liberal contribution made.

"Mr. John Bright in his letter said that Birmingham had manifested great interest in the struggle in the United States for the overthrow of slavery, and we had expected a kindly co-operation from its inhabitants. Early in the winter I called upon Mr. F. Hine, and with him visited Mr. Arthur Albright, whose name had long been familiar in America as a philanthropist. Mr. Albright entered into our plans and contributed to the funds we were raising. Mr. Hine formed a committee, who performed a very large amount of work to secure the greatest possible results for the singers. Meanwhile Birmingham was experiencing great agitation resulting from meetings of the school-board. Great reforms are usually centred in some locality from which influences issue. It seemed to me that reforms for the more liberal education of children had their centre in this town. School-board meetings were the exciting incidents of the day, and no less a personage than a daughter of the family of Burgess was a member of the board, and sat among the distinguished friends of education. The Rev. R. W. Dale, M.A., the successor of John Angell James, was a leading spirit at these meetings, and famous throughout the midland counties for his advocacy of a school system that should be national rather than sectarian. As we also were furthering work for the better education of the poor, we expected great sympathy, and in this we were not disappointed. The mayor, Mr. Chamberlain, granted us the use of the Town Hall at a reduced rate, and took the chair at our first concert. He also made a felicitous speech, and contributed to our funds. A very large audience greeted us, and the generous co-operation of the inhabitants fully sustained the good name which this great manufacturing town bears in the United States. At the second concert the chairman gave us money for a room, while Mr. Dale arranged a large missionary meeting, which was addressed by Mr. Dickerson on the Sabbath. And thus ended the midland county campaign, which was at once fraught with our bitterest trials and our greatest financial success."

## CHAPTER XI.

### THE CLOSING OF THE CAMPAIGN.

"'Way over in the Egypt land
You shall gain the victory.
'Way over in the Egypt land,
You shall gain the day.
March on, and you shall gain the victory,
March on, and you shall gain the day."—*Slave Song.*

FROM Jerusalem the doctor and I proceeded to Port Said, with the intent of passing through the Suez Canal to the confines of the Red Sea. As we neared the locality where it is presumed the Israelites crossed, the doctor observed that, judging from the slave songs he had heard in which there was mention of "Egypt Land," of Moses smiting the water, and the drowning of "ole Pharaoh," he was led to believe that the analogy between the bondage of Israel and that of the American slave had familiarized the Freedmen more with Egypt than with any other portion of Africa, and indeed he believed that Egypt would be an attractive field of missionary labour for the ex-slave. As I had ever entertained the wish that the missionary might be sent at once into the arena of the equatorial hunting grounds, from whence so many millions of slaves had been bought or stolen, I made him no answer. On nearing Cairo he resumed the subject by calling my attention to the complexion of the Egyptians.

"They look," he said, "generally just like American Freedmen; they are intelligent, and very eager to acquire different languages. They represent all the tribes of Africa, and if you had here a missionary school, like the Hampton Normal Institute, or like the Protestant College at Beirut, you could supply the agencies needful for the evangelization of the equatorial regions. The Moslems," he went on to say, "had gone down from Egypt and Barbary and made proselytes of a people in Africa occupying an amount of territory equal in extent to Europe."

He then took a map and explained to me how already a railway was being constructed along the Nile to Khartoum, a point half-way to the equator, and assured me that in time the road would be extended to Gondokoro, less than five degrees latitude north, and in close proximity to a lake system said to be seven hundred miles in extent.

"As one great essential," he continued, "for the development of Egyptian civilization is coal, which exists in abundance in the territory south of the Great Lakes, there is reason to hope this road will be completed. Then your missionary can go from London to Lake

Albert N'yanza, in the very heart of the slave-hunting grounds, in nine days, or from Alexandria in three."

"Egypt," I said, "must be the New York of Africa, while its Chicago will doubtless be established on one of the great equatorial lakes."

"Yes," rejoined the doctor; "and as in America it is entirely compatible to educate missionaries at Bangor or Andover to labour at Mobile or New Orleans, so it is equally simple to train workers in Egypt for Central Africa. We cannot at present do the details needful for the evangelization of the Soudan on the ground. Teachers and preachers for that people, however, may be prepared where the climate and civilization is favourable, and these may go out to teach and evangelize."

"But," I said, "I have just been reading Captain Speke, and find that when he stood at Ripon Falls, on the shore of the Victoria N'yanza, he was led to exclaim, 'What a place *this* would be for missionaries! If farming were introduced by them they might have hundreds of pupils.' I also find that during the extreme heat experienced in these regions the thermometer only rose to 92°, while the mean temperature for the year was estimated at 68°. Why would it not be best to go at once either by Zanzibar or Egypt to these latitudes, and found your Chicago; or, as I may more fittingly say, establish your missionary college?"

"There is no stable government to protect you," he

said, "or civilization upon which to build your school in the Soudan, as yet. In Egypt, however, you have a base for operations; you should learn a lesson from the apostles, who worked on the tide of civilization!"

"These things are doubtless true," I replied; "but great success has been achieved by English and German missionaries on the Gold Coast; while at Sierra Leone, Liberia, and Cape Palmas, the English and Americans number their converts by thousands. At Cape Colony, Kaffraria, Bechuana, Natal, and other southern regions a great work has been accomplished by missionary societies of different Protestant countries; while missions at Madagascar, an island off the south-east coast of Africa, have as many as 67,388 church members. It is not so much *where* in Africa work should be done, as how we can find the men and the means to do it. There are many healthy lands, located very favourably, awaiting missionary labours."

By this time we had reached Cairo, where we visited the mission established by a daughter of Archbishop Whately, and also one sustained by the United Presbyterians of America; but these agencies were utterly inadequate to keep pace with the rapid growth of Egyptian civilization, which is fast extending itself towards equatorial Africa. The doctor and I took a fancy to make our journey to the Pyramids at a time which would enable us to reach them about dawn of day, and, ascending to the summit of Cheops, we endeavoured to pledge ourselves anew to labour for African evangelization, wherever the most open and urgent fields for effort should present themselves, and that, as all missionary labour for the Freedmen of America looked towards Africa, we should study diligently how best to fill the hand with heaven's blessing that Ethiopia was stretching out to God. When we had done this, it was understood that I should, in narrating the closing scenes in the Jubilee Singers' Campaign for £10,000, speak of some of the hopeful characteristics developed in their journeyings, and keep in mind that the work they represented would never be ended till the whole of Africa was brought to Christ. .

"As to the singers themselves," I said, "they found that on the whole it was easier for them to do their work in Great Britain than it had been in America. The distance to be travelled from town to town when giving concerts was not so great. The climate was not cold in winter, while they were never hindered by ice or snow. The fogs and dampness made it needful for them to exercise great care in dull or rainy weather; but apart from this there was little to embarrass them. Few of them suffered from sickness, and at the end of the campaign they appeared as strong and courageous as ever. The attentions they received had become so common that they were not especially flattered; indeed, so much of this was

## THE CLOSING OF THE CAMPAIGN. 187

bestowed after they had exerted themselves to the utmost to do well, that they were exhausted in receiving it, and it often became a rather irksome addition to their labours. There is an amount of attention that serves as a stimulus, and, indeed, as a healthy support; but when a certain limit is reached, every excess is a burden. Popular men, and women as well, doubtless often suffer more from undue attentions than unknown persons from a lack of notice. A wise providence seems to balance our circumstances so as to give to every man a penny. I think there were many hopeful characteristics developed in the students during both their American and European campaigns. One was a desire to do their work well: they generally fully realized how much depended upon that. Another was a disposition to convince people that the Freedmen could appreciate the efforts put forth for their advancement, and that such efforts, so far as they were concerned, had not been expended in vain. They were also neat in their habits, and careful in their use of language. I never heard an immodest word from one of them, or observed an impropriety of deportment in the intercourse between the gentlemen and ladies of the party, during the two years I was associated with them; and this, I think, is as much as could be said of any eleven young people born *out* of slavery. The most of them were careful of their clothing, and saving of money, while their great ambition seemed to be for advancement in their studies. Few, if any of them, were content with their attainments, and I think none of them would knowingly do anything to weaken the confidence of their many thousand generous friends. Mr. White's singleness of purpose and rare taste was of great assistance to them in almost every respect; while the counsels and care of Miss Gilbert, a daughter of Dr. Gilbert of Fredonia, New York, were of constant assistance in all matters pertaining to their public life. The young men often mentioned in their brief public addresses how very desirable it would be to prepare the Freedmen for missionaries to Africa; and the last time I heard Mr. Dickerson speak, he gave the impression that he was about to enter upon studies to fit himself for the work of a missionary in that land.

"As to the closing work of the campaign," I continued, "it embraced work done in Wales and the south of England. Mr. Halley and Miss Gilbert had by this time so far recovered as to be enabled to proceed with their labours, and the pressure of business was more easily borne. Mr. J. B. Graham, of Newport, in Monmouthshire, received us when we came down from Birmingham, and the large Victoria Hall was crowded to its utmost with people waiting to welcome the singers. We had often heard it said that the Welsh were not only exceedingly fond of

## The Closing of the Campaign. 189

music, but filled with religious devotion as well; and what we experienced in Newport fully justified this report. As we only proposed to visit four towns in this Principality, we went from Newport to Swansea for our next engagement. On our arrival we were honoured with much attention at the Maxwell Arms Hotel, and received visits from prominent townspeople. The audience at Swansea was very large, and the interest awakened by the singers unusual. During the intermission I made a statement of our success and necessities, telling the people that we wished to secure money for rooms. The chairman, after endorsing our mission, walked down through the audience and collected from one and another more than sufficient for the furnishing of one, to bear the name of Swansea. The weather was fine, and during Saturday we visited Oystermouth Castle and other places of interest. On Tuesday we were engaged at Cardiff, where the Rev. D. Howell, of the Established Church, had favoured me with assistance. In him we found a representative of the genuine vicar. He looked after the temporal as well as the spiritual wants of his flock; and the kindness he manifested to poor people calling on him for assistance completely won my heart. We were also indebted to Mr. Jones, proprietor of a large book warehouse and printing establishment, who did all in his power to make our concert a success, and insisted on undertaking the sale of our tickets gratis. Our concert was given in the Temperance Town Chapel, where every precaution had been taken to avoid a crush of people, on account of the great demand for tickets. The mayor took the chair, and at the intermission, the audience being in a most generous mood, some one proposed that boxes be passed to gather up contributions for a room to bear the name of Cardiff. A very willing response was made, the collection amounting to nearly enough for two. A concert was also given at Merthyr Tydvil.

"If our engagements had allowed, there is reason to believe that we might have secured a much larger harvest among the very appreciative and kindly disposed people of these towns.

"Mr. Samuel Budgett, of Bristol, a son of 'The Successful Merchant,' the history of whose benevolent acts is well known in America, had heard the students in London. I had applied to him for co-operation early in the winter, and most of the excellent arrangements for this town were completed under his supervision. Leading citizens gave their patronage, and the mayor promised to take the chair. As Mr. George Müller's orphanage is situated on the Ashley Downs, near Bristol, I had hoped that the students might get some adequate idea of the method of his work, as a suggestion to them during future labours. I therefore made the acquaintance of Mr. Müller, and stated to him the object of our enterprise. It was on the Sabbath, and he had been preaching to a newly-established church. I remember particularly the impression he made upon me respecting his business capacity. I thought he would have been as distinguished if he had been a banker or merchant as he now was as a philanthropist. His mind is very clear and well trained, and the steps he takes in whatever he does are judiciously chosen. When I saw the five massive stone buildings on a hill overlooking a beautiful stretch of open country, and observed the neatness and order of all their appointments, and learned the successive steps he pursued in raising the money, purchasing the ground, and putting up the buildings, one after another, till he had made ample room for two thousand children, I understood that his prayers were accompanied with superior sagacity. He said to me that his object had been to make it known how God answered prayer, and that the five buildings were monuments of God's faithfulness; that by them it could be seen that even in our day God is a present help to aid in the accomplishment of great things for Himself. Mr. Müller also told me that the income of the orphanage during one year equalled £50,000, or $250,000. Some days after this interview Mrs. Müller wrote to me for the purpose of furthering our wishes respecting a visit of the Jubilee Singers, but other engagements prevented its fulfilment. The Rev. Dr. Doudney had heard the singers in London and very kindly wrote an article in his own name, and published it in one of the papers. He also took the chair in the absence of the mayor at the Victoria Rooms, the first night a concert was given in Clifton. Mr. Cook, a young man in the employment of Mr. Budgett, volunteered much service in furthering our arrangements, and generous citizens subscribed money for furnishing two rooms in the Jubilee Hall—one to bear the name of Colston and the other Livingstone. Our visit to Bristol was one replete with encouraging circumstances, and the proceeds of the concerts large, considering the size of the hall where they took place. Although we had many generous promises of co-operation if we would visit other large towns in the west of England, we only closed with the overtures made by the citizens of Bath. Here Mr. Henry Denning, a gentleman who devotes much time as a lay preacher for the elevation of the masses, proffered his aid, and on account of my illness assumed all the responsibility of the work. After the concert, which was a pleasant success, he kindly accompanied the students to the hot springs and grounds made famous since the Roman conquest. He also took us into the abbey church, and devoted much attention to explaining the historic incidents the city afforded. Here we saw a statue of the world-renowned Beau Brummell. From Bath the students went to London, to be again welcomed by Mr. Spurgeon, according to arrangements made the summer

## THE CLOSING OF THE CAMPAIGN. 193

before. When they went forth they had little save the blessings of the London people; when they returned they brought their sheaves with them. They had commenced working for £6,000; they had returned with nearly ten. Although the great preacher had so many and varied duties, he did not forget his promise of books for the Fisk University, but brought his literary sheaves with him to the concert. Mr. Blackshaw, his secretary, had consented a second time to attend to the essential details of advertising, and a second time the house was densely crowded. Many well-known persons were present, among whom was the Rev. Dr. Moffat, also the Rev. R. Balgarnie, of Scarborough. The programme was one of much interest, and Mr. Spurgeon was happy, as he ever is, in his remarks. During the intermission a large parcel containing about twenty volumes of his sermons and other works was brought to the platform, when Mr. Spurgeon in a felicitous speech presented them to the Fisk University. In accepting them on behalf of that institution, I endeavoured to assure him and the audience that we fully appreciated how much men like Mr. Beecher and Mr. Spurgeon had to do with the great success we had achieved, and how we should ever remember with pleasure the way in which the Prime Minister of Great Britain and the greatest preacher of the nineteenth century had honoured the humble endeavours of a few negro children, who were labouring for the recovery of a people that had been hated and wronged. Dr. Moffat, the veteran African missionary, gave expression to great hopefulness that the wonderful interest manifested in these coloured people would result in lasting benefits; and throughout the entire evening there was a heartiness of interest fitted to impress us with the thought that we were experiencing a foretaste of the time when the 'Redeemed of the Lord shall return with singing unto Zion.' The proceeds of the concert were considerably in excess of the one given at the Tabernacle on a former occasion; while not only Mr. Spurgeon but also his people have written their names very high in the annals of the uprising of the Freedmen in America. There were now only a few engagements to fulfil before the farewell concert. Two of these were at Brighton, where the students were to spend the Sabbath, and sing in the great Dome on Monday and Wednesday. Messrs. Albrighton and Beves had fully informed the people of the students' cause and previous success. The mayor, Mr. Alderman Brigden, occupied the chair on one of the evenings, and a large company of visitors and friends at this extensive watering-place were present, and appreciative. In the many full reports given in the papers especial mention was made of Miss Maggie Porter, whose rendering of, 'If I were a voice,' during the last weeks of our concerts, attracted much attention. Another concert, and the only one I will speak of, was given at Southampton, through the kindness of the Rev. Septimus March, who had obtained for us the use of the large lecture-hall at the Scientific Institute, and had given his influence and labours to awaken an interest among the people of his town. As it not unfrequently happened, the crowd of people was so great that long before the time announced for opening they broke over the barriers in the entrance of the building, causing much confusion among the different classes of ticket-holders. The service, however, was in every way a success."

"But," inquired the doctor, "have you not failed to tell me about a great number of towns where you were well received, and of churches and individuals who gave you assurances and money?"

"To be sure," I said. "Sir Sidney Waterlow, Lord Mayor of London, told me in 1873 that he would take the chair if I would gather a public meeting for the benefit of our mission; while Mr. Alderman Lusk, M.P., the present Lord Mayor, promised to preside on one occasion, and would have done so had he not been unexpectedly detained by a military banquet at the Mansion House, held in honour of Sir Garnet Wolseley. Many Sunday-schools gave money for the library, while donations of books and pictures were frequent. It has only been my purpose to mention some of the more noteworthy events in the campaign; and as I now recall the honoured names associated with them they seem to span themselves above me like a galaxy of stars. The Queen of Britain lends her ear, the Prime Minister listens again and again with sympathetic affection. Dukes and earls, lords and ladies, stars of the first magnitude, are there. Members of Parliament by scores, mayors and councillors, dignitaries of the Church, philosophers, scholars, philanthropists, musicians, bankers, merchants, citizens, and a milky way of millions of working people are all there, while the Star of Bethlehem shines over them all—a firmament that may indeed be a lasting inspiration to the Black man as he seeks for advancement. We have now come," I went on to say, "to the closing concert of the campaign, at Exeter Hall, which yielded us greater returns from the sale of tickets than any other given in the country. It was the goal to which our eyes had turned for many days. There were present the Rev. Henry Allon, D.D., to whom the singers had been especially commended before their departure from America; the Rev. Newman Hall, whose letter in the *New York Independent* had proved of incalculable value, not only in overcoming prejudice in the United States, but also in aiding us in raising funds; and (as was most becoming) the Right Hon. the Earl of Shaftesbury, who presided on their first appearance in London, was present and occupied the chair. 'We need not characterize the singing,' says the *English Independent;* 'but, recalling the first appearance of the singers after their arrival in England, we could not but note that, although they must have been well-nigh surfeited with applause, they are as natural and unaffected now as at the beginning of the campaign, while their execution seems to have gained in precision.'

"At the interval between the two parts of the concert Dr. Allon made a statement of the results of the campaign, telling the audience that, in addition to the amount needed for the construction of Jubilee Hall, the singers had secured £400 by special donations, for furnishing students' dormitories at an average cost of £10 each; that £250 had been given towards a library, and books by Mr. Gladstone, Dean Stanley, Mr. Spurgeon, Thomas Nelson, and many others. Members of the Society of Friends, through the efforts of Mr. E. R. Ransome, had contributed £231 for the purchase of a set of philosophical apparatus, in addition to a donation of books. Hull had given to the University an oil painting of Wilberforce; Mr. Bradford, the marine artist, a beautiful painting; while Mr. F. Havill the artist, had given two portraits in oil, one of David Livingstone and the other of Mr. White, the treasurer of the University, and was now at work on a life-sized painting of the Jubilee Singers. Dr. Allon concluded by giving an account of the more prominent events of the campaign, ending with commendations and assurances fitted alike to sanction what we had done and to encourage the British people who had so kindly aided us.

"Mr. Ransome, on behalf of the Society of Friends, was present, bearing gifts; and after a statement to the effect that there were still two million persons held in slavery by professing Christians, he introduced his two little daughters, who, amid the hearty applause of the audience, presented the singers with the £231 mentioned above. Mr. Holmes, in acknowledging the gift, closed with the following words:—

"'You have nobly responded to our appeal for £6,000, and have given us £10,000, and we feel sure the foundation of Jubilee Hall, which was laid last spring with American greenbacks, will be capped with British gold. (Laughter and cheers.) We hope in that University a noble work will be accomplished. We hope that we who live in the Southern States of America will be able to prove to you that we are worthy of the liberty which, through the influence of good people and by the blessing of God, we now enjoy. (Cheers.) We hope that men and women will be educated there who shall go to Africa—that country which has so long been in bondage and sin—and carry the glad tidings, and tell the Africans that there is a God for them. We ask you, as we leave you, that you will remember us in your sympathies and prayers to God, that we may be successful in the work which we have undertaken. By the assistance of the good people of

## THE CLOSING OF THE CAMPAIGN. 199

England and America, and by our own efforts, we hope by the blessing of God to get, before many years, even Africa to praise God and serve Him as you do. (Applause.)

"At the close of the singing, which had been received with expressions of continued interest, Lord Shaftesbury said,—

"'Before this meeting closes, you will, I am sure, allow me to express to these young people the delight with which you have received them in this country, and the regret with which you part from them; and you will permit me also to express your deep sympathy with all the sorrows they have undergone, and with the success that, under the blessing of Almighty God, they have been enabled to achieve. And now we can do it with great comfort and free speech, as before we had a free heart, for our brethren in America; we have now wiped away the cursed reproach of slavery, and we can now rejoice with them in wishing well for the advancement of the human race. As you listened to the songs they sing did you observe the high, the tender, hallowed sentiment that pervaded all that they expressed? Did you observe, in these people singing to you the songs of their captivity, that the prayer came from their hearts to God to keep them "from sinking down"? He has not only kept them from sinking down, but raised them in His mercy; and now they stand before you fit to compete with the very best of all the human race. (Cheers.) See how, the moment the pressure was removed, they have come forth and have been the means not only of exalting themselves but all their brethren who have been so long trodden down in the lowest depths of human misery. It is a glorious manifestation of moral virtue, and will teach us, I hope, henceforward to know that there is no distinction of heart, although there may be distinction of colour, and that God has made of one blood all the nations of the whole world. (Cheers.) I assume, then, that I may address these young people, and say to them on your behalf, and on behalf of the whole kingdom of England, that our affection and respect will follow them wherever they go through all the period of time; and I pray Almighty God that we may all join them in that blessed eternity, the hope of which sustained them in all their sorrows and all their despair.' (Loud applause.)

"The Doxology was sung by the entire assembly, and Lord Shaftesbury, amid the cheers of the audience, shook hands with each of the singers as they quitted the platform.

"And thus ended the Campaign for £10,000. The students tarried in England a few weeks before leaving for America, completing some arrangements for themselves, and taking a kindly farewell of friends for whom they had formed endearing attachments. With the exception of Mr. Dickerson, who remained to study

## THE CLOSING OF THE CAMPAIGN. 201

in Edinburgh, those whose homes were in Nashville returned to the Fisk University in time to participate in the commencement exercises.

"They were met at New York on their arrival by General Clinton B. Fisk, the Rev. E. M. Cravath, and Captain Stewart, officers of the Fisk University, who, together with the Rev. George Whipple and the Rev. M. E. Strieby, corresponding secretaries of the American Missionary Association, welcomed them home; while at Nashville formal resolutions expressive of thanks for the services rendered were adopted, and a copy of them supplied to each of the members of the company.

"'We have followed the singers,' said the trustees of the University, 'with feelings of the deepest interest and sympathy, and have rejoiced in their patient industry, their zeal, their devotion to their great art, their purity and their humility, their great success, and the high honour they have achieved for themselves and for the people for whom they went out. No one can estimate the vast amount of prejudice against the race which has perished under the spell of their marvellous music. Wherever they have gone they have proclaimed to the hearts of men in a most effective way, and with unanswerable logic, the brotherhood of the race.'

"That the blessings of this brotherhood may be co-extensive with the human family, and that the influences for good promoted by the Jubilee Singers may increase till the last vestige of prejudice against a people—'Guilty of a skin not coloured like our own'—is removed, and that Africa itself may rise and shine, its light being come,—shall, with ever-increasing faith, become the prayer of one who in the 'Singing Campaign' has been permitted to see 'the glory and the coming of the Lord.'"

THE END.

# JUBILEE SONGS.

# PREFACE TO THE MUSIC.

In giving these melodies to the world in a tangible form, it seems desirable to say a few words about them as judged from a musical stand-point. It is certain that the critic stands completely disarmed in their presence. He must not only recognize their immense power over audiences which include many people of the highest culture, but, if he be not thoroughly encased in prejudice, he must yield a tribute of admiration on his own part, and acknowledge that these songs touch a chord which the most consummate art fails to reach. Something of this result is doubtless due to the singers as well as to their melodies. The excellent rendering of the Jubilee Band is made more effective and the interest is intensified by the comparison of their former state of slavery and degradation with the present prospects and hopes of their race, which crowd upon every listener's mind during the singing of their songs. Yet the power is chiefly in the songs themselves, and hence a brief analysis of them will be of interest.

Their origin is unique. They are never "composed" after the manner of ordinary music, but spring into life, ready made, from the white heat of religious fervor during some protracted meeting in church or camp. They come from no musical cultivation whatever, but are the simple, ecstatic utterances of wholly untutored minds. From so unpromising a source we could reasonably expect only such a mass of crudities as would be unendurable to the cultivated ear. On the contrary, however, the cultivated listener confesses to a new charm, and to a power never before felt, at least in its kind. What can we infer from this but that the child-like, receptive minds of these unfortunates were wrought upon with a true inspiration, and that this gift was bestowed upon them by an ever-watchful Father, to quicken the pulses of life, and to keep them from the state of hopeless apathy into which they were in danger of falling.

A technical analysis of these melodies shows some interesting facts. The first peculiarity that strikes the attention is in the rhythm. This is often complicated, and sometimes strikingly original. But although so new and strange, it is most remarkable that these effects are so extremely satisfactory. We see few cases of what theorists call *mis-form*, although the student of musical composition is likely to fall into that error long after he has mastered the leading principles of the art.

Another noticeable feature of the songs is the entire absence of triple time, or three-part measure among them. The reason for this is doubtless to be found in the beating of the foot and the swaying of the body which are such frequent accompaniments of the singing. These motions are in even measure, and in perfect time; and so it will be found that however broken and seemingly irregular the movement of the music, it is always capable of the most exact measurement. In other words, its irregularities invariably conform to the "higher law" of the perfect rhythmic flow.

It is a coincidence worthy of note that more than half the melodies in this collection are in the same scale as that in which Scottish music is written; that is, with the fourth and seventh tones omitted. The fact that the music of the ancient Greeks is also said to have been written in this scale, suggests an interesting inquiry as to whether it may not be a peculiar language of nature, or a simpler alphabet than the ordinary diatonic scale, in which the uncultivated mind finds its easiest expression.

The variety of forms presented in these songs is truly surprising, when their origin is considered. This diversity is greater than the listener would at first be likely to suppose. The frequent recurrence of one particular effect, viz.: that given on the last syllable of the word "chariot" in the first line of "Swing Low," conveys an impression of sameness which is not justified by the general structure of the songs. The themes are quite as distinct and varied as in the case of more pretentious compositions.

The public may feel assured that the music herein given is entirely correct. It was taken down from the singing of the band, during repeated interviews held for the purpose, and no line or phrase was introduced that did not receive full indorsement from the singers. Some of the phrases and turns in the melodies are so peculiar that the listener might not unreasonably suppose them to be incapable of exact representation by ordinary musical characters. It is found, however, that they all submit to the laws of musical language, and if they are sung or played exactly as written, all the characteristic effects will be reproduced.

THEO. F. SEWARD,
ORANGE, N. J.

## JUBILEE SONGS.*

It will be observed that in most of these songs the first strain is of the nature of a chorus or refrain, which is to be sung after each verse. The return to this chorus should be made without breaking the time.

In some of the verses the syllables do not correspond exactly to the notes in the music. The adaptation is so easy that it was thought best to leave it to the skill of the singer rather than to confuse the eye by too many notes. The music is in each case carefully adapted to the first verse. Whatever changes may be necessary in singing the remaining verses will be found to involve no difficulty.

### Nobody knows the Trouble I see, Lord!

No-bo-dy knows the trouble I see, Lord, No-bo-dy knows the

trou-ble I see, No-bo-dy knows the trouble I see, Lord,

FINE.
No-bo-dy knows like Je-sus. 1. Broth-ers, will you

pray for me, Brothers, will you pray for me, Brothers, will you

D. C.
pray for me, And help me to drive old Sa-tan a-way.

2. Sisters, will you pray for me, &c.
3. Mothers, will you pray for me, &c.
4. Preachers, will you pray for me, &c.

---

* A separate edition of these Songs, in large type, is published by Messrs. BIGLOW & MAIN, 425 Broome Street, New York. Price, 25 cents. For sale also at the rooms of the Am. Mis. Association.

## Swing low, sweet Chariot.

# Room Enough.

2 Oh, mourners, don't stay away.
   *Cho.*—For the Bible says there's room enough, &c.

3 Oh, sinners, don't stay away.
   *Cho.*—For the angel says there's room enough, &c.

4 Oh, children, don't stay away.
   *Cho.*—For Jesus says there's room enough, &c.

\* The peculiar accent here makes the words sound thus: "rooma nough."

## 210 — Redeemed.

* Attention is called to this characteristic manner of connecting the last strain with the chorus in the D. C.

## 212. Children, we all shall be Free.

*(Chil-dren, we all shall be free, Chil-dren, we all shall be free, Children, we all shall be free, When the Lord shall appear.)*

1. We want no cowards in our band,
   That from their colors fly,
   We call for val-iant-heart-ed men,
   That are not a-fraid to die.

2. We see the pilgrim as he lies,
   With glory in his soul;
   To Heaven he lifts his longing eyes,
   And bids this world adieu.
   Cho.—Children, we all shall be free, &c.

3. Give ease to the sick, give sight to the blind,
   Enable the cripple to walk;
   He'll raise the dead from under the earth,
   And give them permission to fly.
   Cho.—Children, we all shall be free, &c.

\* The words, "On Jordan's stormy banks I stand," are sometimes sung to this strain.

# Roll, Jordan, Roll.

2. Oh, preachers, you ought t'have been there, &c.
3. Oh, sinners, you ought, &c.
4. Oh, mourners, you ought, &c.
5. Oh, seekers, you ought, &c.
6. Oh, mothers, you ought, &c.
7. Oh, children, you ought, &c.

# 214. Turn back Pharaoh's Army.

SOLO. *Moderato.*

1. Gwine to write to Mas-sa Je-sus, To send some valiant soldier,
2. If you want your souls converted, You'd better be a-praying,
3. You say you are a soldier, Fighting for your Saviour,
4. When the children were in bondage, They cried unto the Lord,
5. When Mo-ses smote the wa-ter, The children all passed over,
6. When Pharaoh crossed the water, The waters came to-gether,

CHORUS. *Faster.*

1. To turn back Pharaoh's army, Hal-le-lu! To turn back Pharaoh's
2. To turn back Pharaoh's army, Hal-le-lu! To turn back, &c.
3. To turn back Pharaoh's army, Hal-le-lu! To turn back, &c.
4. He turned back Pharaoh's army, Hal-le-lu! He turned back, &c.
5. And turned back Pharaoh's army, Hal-le-lu! And turned back, &c.
6. And drowned ole Pharaoh's army, Hal-le-lu! And drowned ole, &c.

ar-my, Hal-le-lu-jah! To turn back Pharaoh's

ar-my, Hal-le-lu! To turn back Pharaoh's ar-my, Hal-le-

lu-jah! To turn back Pharaoh's ar-my, Hal-le-lu!

# I'm a Rolling.

* Return to the beginning in exact time.

216 Didn't my Lord deliver Daniel.

\* Go on without pause, leaving out two beats of the measure.

## I'll hear the Trumpet Sound.

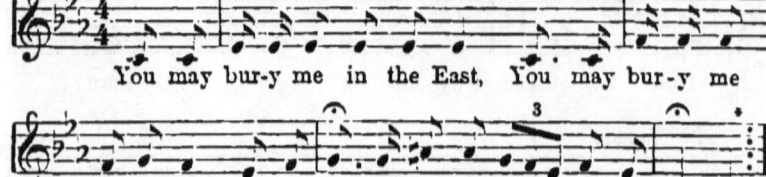

2. Father Gabriel in that day,
He'll take wings and fly away,
For to hear the trumpet sound
In that morning.
You may bury him in the East,
You may bury him in the West;
But he'll hear the trumpet sound,
In that morning.

  *Cho.*—In that morning, &c.

3. Good old christians in that day,
They'll take wings and fly away,&c.
  *Cho.*—In that morning, &c.

4. Good old preachers in that day,
They'll take wings and fly away,&c.
  *Cho.*—In that morning, &c.

5. In that dreadful Judgment day,
I'll take wings and fly away, &c.
  *Cho.*—In that morning, &c.

\* Repeat the music of the first strain for all the verses but the first.

## Rise, Mourners.*

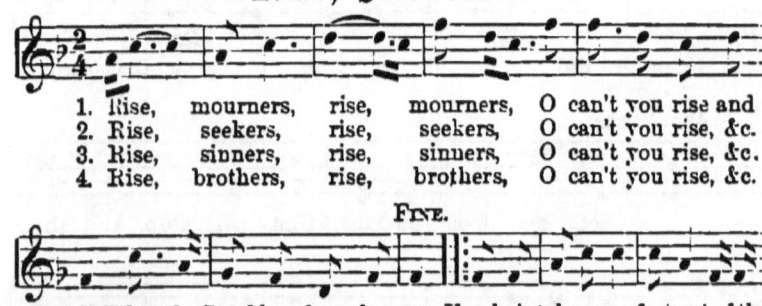

1. Rise, mourners, rise, mourners, O can't you rise and
2. Rise, seekers, rise, seekers, O can't you rise, &c.
3. Rise, sinners, rise, sinners, O can't you rise, &c.
4. Rise, brothers, rise, brothers, O can't you rise, &c.

tell, What the Lord has done for you. Yes, he's taken my feet out of the

mi - ry clay, And he's placed them on the right side of my Father.

\* This hymn is sung with great unction while "seekers" are going forward to the altar.

# I've just come from the Fountain. 219

1. I've just come from the fountain, I've just come from the fountain, Lord! I've just come from the fountain, His name's so sweet.
2. Been drinking from the fountain, Been drinking, &c.

CHORUS.

O brothers, I love Jesus, O brothers, I love Jesus, O brothers, I love Jesus, His name's so sweet.

3. I found free grace at the fountain,
I found free grace, &c.
   *Cho.*—O preachers, I love Jesus, &c.

4. My soul's set free at the fountain,
My soul's set free, &c.
   *Cho.*—O sinners, I love Jesus, &c.

\* The Tenors usually sing the melody from this point.

12

## 220. Gwine to ride up in the Chariot.

mer—cy on me, And I hope I'll join the band.

2. Gwine to meet my brother there, Sooner, &c.
   *Cho.*—O Lord, have mercy, &c.
3. Gwine to chatter with the Angels, Sooner, &c.
   *Cho.*—O Lord, have mercy, &c.
4. Gwine to meet my massa Jesus, Sooner, &c.
   *Cho.*—O Lord, have mercy, &c.
5. Gwine to walk and talk with Jesus, Sooner, &c.
   *Cho.*—O Lord, have mercy, &c.

## We'll Die in the Field.

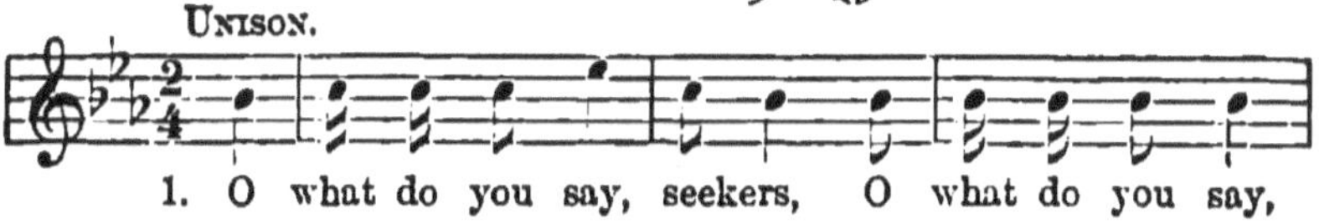

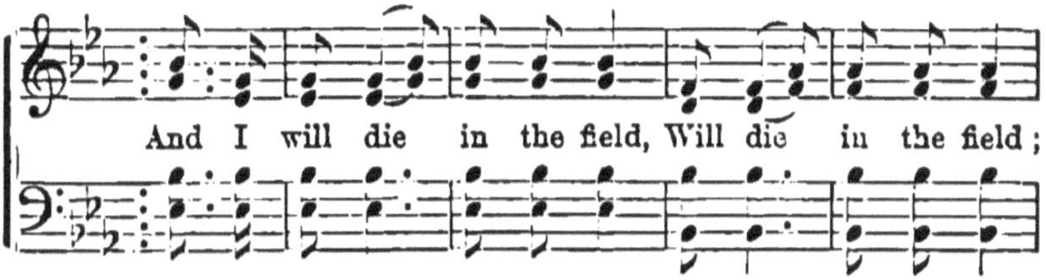

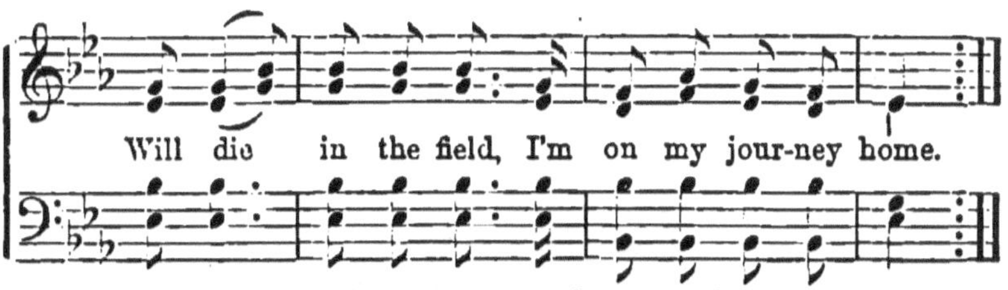

1. O what do you say, seekers, O what do you say, seekers; O what do you say, seekers, A-bout the Gospel war? And I will die in the field, Will die in the field; Will die in the field, I'm on my jour-ney home.

2. O what do you say, brothers, &c.
3. O what do you say, christians, &c.
4. O what do you say, preachers, &c.

## Children, you'll be called on.

1. Chil-dren, you'll be called on  To march in  the field of
2. Preachers, you'll be called on  To march in  the field, &c.
3. Sin-ners, you'll be called on  To march in  the field, &c.
4. Seek-ers, you'll be called on  To march in  the field, &c.
5. Christians, you'll be called on  To march in  the field, &c.

bat-tle, When this war-fare'll be end-ed, Hal-le-lu.

**CHORUS.**

When this war-fare'll be end-ed, I'm a sol-dier of the

ju-bi-lee, This warfare'll be ended, I'm a soldier of the cross.

## Give me Jesus.

1. O when I come to die, O when I come to die, O
2. In the morning when I rise, In the morning when I rise, &c.
3. Dark midnight was my cry, Dark midnight was my cry, &c.
4. I heard the mourner say, I heard the mourner say, &c.

when I come to die—Give me Je-sus, Give me Je-

sus, Give me Je-sus, You may have all this world, Give me Je-sus.

# The Rocks and the Mountains.

2. Doubter, doubter, give up your heart to God,
   And you shall have a new hiding-place that day.
   Oh, the rocks, &c.

3. Mourner, mourner, give up your heart to God, &c.
4. Sinner, sinner, give up your heart to God, &c.
5. Sister, sister, give up your heart to God, &c.
6. Mother, mother, give up your heart to God, &c.
7. Children, children, give up your heart to God, &c.

# Go down, Moses.

2. Thus saith the Lord, bold Moses said,
    Let my people go ;
  If not I'll smite your first-born dead,
    Let my people go.
      Go down, Moses, &c.

3. No more shall they in bondage toil,
    Let my people go ;
  Let them come out with Egypt's spoil,
    Let my people go.
      Go down, Moses, &c.

4. When Israel out of Egypt came,
   Let my people go;
   And left the proud oppressive land,
   Let my people go.
   Go down, Moses, &c.

5. O, 'twas a dark and dismal night,
   Let my people go;
   When Moses led the Israelites,
   Let my people go.
   Go down, Moses, &c.

6. 'Twas good old Moses and Aaron, too,
   Let my people go;
   'Twas they that led the armies through,
   Let my people go.
   Go down, Moses, &c.

7. The Lord told Moses what to do,
   Let my people go;
   To lead the children of Israel through,
   Let my people go.
   Go down, Moses, &c.

8. O come along, Moses, you'll not get lost,
   Let my people go;
   Stretch out your rod and come across,
   Let my people go.
   Go down, Moses, &c.

9. As Israel stood by the water side,
   Let my people go;
   At the command of God it did divide,
   Let my people go.
   Go down, Moses, &c.

10. When they had reached the other shore,
    Let my people go;
    They sang a song of triumph o'er,
    Let my people go.
    Go down, Moses, &c.

11. Pharaoh said he would go across,
    Let my people go;
    But Pharaoh and his host were lost,
    Let my people go.
    Go down, Moses, &c.

12. O, Moses, the cloud shall cleave the way,
    Let my people go;
    A fire by night, a shade by day,
    Let my people go.
    Go down, Moses, &c.

13. You'll not get lost in the wilderness,
    Let my people go;
    With a lighted candle in your breast,
    Let my people go.
    Go down, Moses, &c.

14. Jordan shall stand up like a wall,
    Let my people go;
    And the walls of Jericho shall fall,
    Let my people go.
    Go down, Moses, &c.

15. Your foes shall not before you stand,
    Let my people go;
    And you'll possess fair Canaan's land,
    Let my people go.
    Go down, Moses, &c.

16. 'Twas just about in harvest time,
    Let my people go;
    When Joshua led his host divine,
    Let my people go.
    Go down, Moses, &c.

17. O let us all from bondage flee,
    Let my people go;
    And let us all in Christ be free,
    Let my people go.
    Go down, Moses, &c.

18. We need not always weep and moan,
    Let my people go;
    And wear these slavery chains forlorn,
    Let my people go.
    Go down, Moses, &c.

19. This world's a wilderness of woe,
    Let my people go;
    O, let us on to Canaan go,
    Let my people go.
    Go down, Moses, &c.

20. What a beautiful morning that will be,
    Let my people go;
    When time breaks up in eternity,
    Let my people go.
    Go down, Moses, &c.

21. O bretheren, bretheren, you'd better be engaged,
    Let my people go;
    For the devil he's out on a big rampage,
    Let my people go.
    Go down, Moses, &c.

22. The Devil he thought he had me fast,
    Let my people go;
    But I thought I'd break his chains at last,
    Let my people go.
    Go down, Moses, &c.

23. O take yer shoes from off yer feet,
    Let my people go;
    And walk into the golden street,
    Let my people go.
    Go down, Moses, &c.

24. I'll tell you what I likes de best,
    Let my people go;
    It is the shouting Methodist,
    Let my people go.
    Go down, Moses, &c.

25. I do believe without a doubt,
    Let my people go;
    That a Christian has the right to shout,
    Let my people go.
    Go down, Moses, &c.

# Keep me from sinking Down.

3. When I was a mourner just like you;
   Keep me from sinking down:
   I mourned and mourned till I got through;
   Keep me from sinking down.
      Oh, Lord, &c.

4. I bless the Lord I'm gwine to die;
   Keep me from sinking down:
   I'm gwine to judgment by-and-by;
   Keep me from sinking down.
      Oh, Lord, &c.

## I'm a trab'ling to the Grabe.

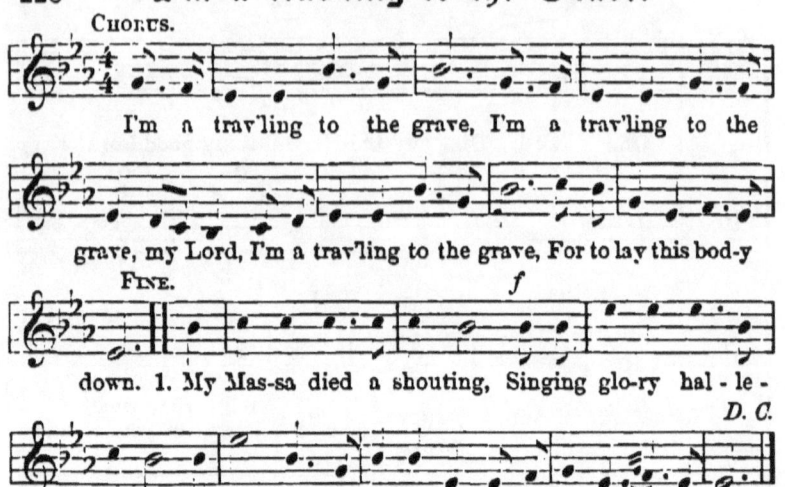

I'm a trav'ling to the grave, I'm a trav'ling to the grave, my Lord, I'm a trav'ling to the grave, For to lay this body down. 1. My Massa died a shouting, Singing glory hal-le-lu-jah, The last word he said to me, Was a-bout Je-ru-sa-lem.

2. My missis died a shouting, &c.
3. My brother died a shouting, &c.
4. My sister died a shouting, &c.

## Many Thousand Gone.

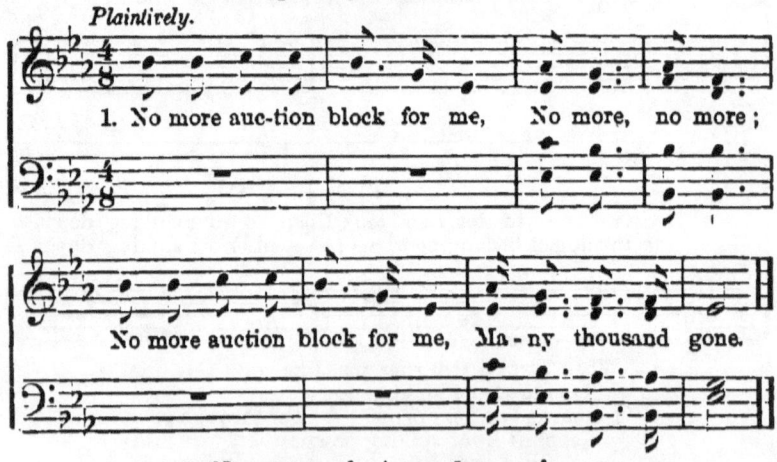

1. No more auc-tion block for me, No more, no more; No more auction block for me, Ma-ny thousand gone.

2. No more peck o' corn for me, &c.
3. No more driver's lash for me, &c.
4. No more pint o' salt for me, &c.
5. No more hundred lash for me, &c.
6. No more mistress' call for me, &c.

## Steal Away.

3. My Lord calls me,
   He calls me by the lightning;
   The trumpet sounds it in my soul:
   I hain't got long to stay here.
       *Cho.* —Steal away, &c.

4. Tombstones are bursting,
   Poor sinners are trembling;
   The trumpet sounds it in my soul:
   I hain't got long to stay here.
       *Cho.*—Steal away, &c.

## He's the Lord of Lords.

Why, He's the Lord of lords, And the King of kings, Why Je-sus Christ is the first and the last, No one can work like Him.

1. I will not let you go, my Lord; No one can work like Him, Until you come and bless my soul, No one can work like Him.

2. For Paul and Silas bound in jail,
  No one can work like Him;
  The Christians prayed both night and day,
  No one can work like Him.
    Cho.—Why, He's the Lord of lords, &c.

3. I wish those mourners would believe,
  No one can work like Him,
  That Jesus is ready to receive,
  No one can work like Him.
    Cho.—Why, He's the Lord of lords, &c.

## Judgment Day is rolling Round.

Judgment, Judgment, Judgment day is rolling around; Judgment, Judgment, O how I long to go. 1. I've a good old mother in the heaven, my Lord, How I long to go there too, I've a good old mother in the heaven, my Lord, O how I long to go.

2. There's no backsliding in the heaven, my Lord,
   How I long to go there too,
   There's no backsliding in the heaven, my Lord,
   O how I long to go.
   *Cho.*—Judgment, &c.

3. King Jesus sitting in the heaven, my Lord,
   How I long to go there too,
   King Jesus sitting in the heaven, my Lord,
   O how I long to go.
   *Cho.*—Judgment, &c.

4. There's a big camp meeting in the heaven, my Lord,
   How I long to go there too,
   There's a big camp meeting in the heaven, my Lord,
   O how I long to go.
   *Cho.*—Judgment, &c.

## The Gospel Train.

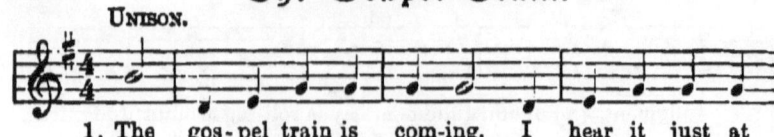

1. The gos-pel train is com-ing, I hear it just at
2. I hear the bell and whis-tle, The com-ing round the
3. No sig-nal for an-oth-er train To fol-low on the

hand, I hear the car wheels moving, And rumbling thro' the land.
curve; She's playing all her steam and pow'r And straining every nerve.
line, O, sinner, you're forever lost, If once you're left be-hind.

Get on board, chil-dren, Get on board, chil-dren, Get on

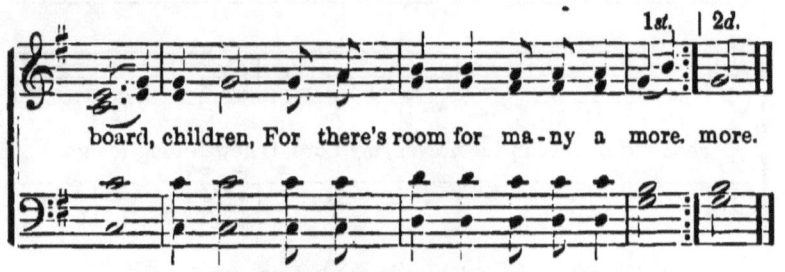

board, children, For there's room for ma-ny a more. more.

4. This is the Christian banner,
   The motto's new and old,
   Salvation and Repentance
   Are burnished there in gold.
   *Cho.*—Get on board, children, &c.

5. She's nearing now the station,
   O, sinner, don't be vain,
   But come and get your ticket,
   And be ready for the train.
   *Cho.*—Get on board, children, &c.

6. The fare is cheap and all can go,
   The rich and poor are there,
   No second-class on board the train,
   No difference in the fare.
   *Cho.*—Get on board, children, &c.

7. There's Moses, Noah and Abraham,
   And all the prophets, too,
   Our friends in Christ are all on board,
   O, what a heavenly crew.
   *Cho.*—Get on board, children, &c.

8. We soon shall reach the station,
   O, how we then shall sing,
   With all the heavenly army,
   We'll make the welkin ring,
   *Cho.*—Get on board, children, &c.

9. We'll shout o'er all our sorrows,
   And sing forever more,
   With Christ and all his army,
   On that celestial shore.
   *Cho.*—Get on board, children, &c.

## Shine, Shine.

2. I'm going to tell God about my trial, &c.
   Oh! my soul's going to shine, &c.
   *Cho.*—Shine, shine, &c.

3. I'm going to walk all about that city, &c.
   Oh! my soul's going to shine, &c.
   *Cho.*—Shine, shine, &c.

## Old Ship of Zion.

In singing the last two verses the music is not to be repeated.

2. She has landed many a thousand, Hallelujah,
She has landed many a thousand, Hallelu,
She has landed many a thousand,
And will land as many a more.   Oh glory, Hallelu.

3. She is loaded down with angels, Hallelujah,
She is loaded down with angels, Hallelu,
And King Jesus is the Captain,
And he'll carry us all home.   Oh glory, Hallelu.

## In the River of Jordan.

1. In the riv-er of Jor-dan John baptized, How I long to be bap-tized; In the riv-er of Jor-dan John bap-tized, To the dy-ing Lamb. Pray on, pray on, pray on, ye mourning souls, Pray on, pray on, un-to the dy-ing Lamb.

2. We baptize all that come by faith,
   How I long to be baptized;
   We baptize all that come by faith,
   To the dying Lamb.
      *Cho.*—Pray on, &c.

3. Here's another one come to be baptized,
   How I long to be baptized;
   Here's another one to be baptized,
   To the dying Lamb.
      *Cho.*—Pray on, &c.

# We'll stand the Storm.

2. She's making for the kingdom,
   We'll anchor, &c.

3. I've a mother in the kingdom,
   We'll anchor, &c.

## I'm so Glad. 237

2. I hope I'll meet my brother there,
   No dying there,
   That used to join with me in prayer,
   No dying there.
   *Cho.*—I'm so glad, &c.

3. I hope I'll meet the preacher there,
   No dying there,
   That used to join with me in prayer,
   No dying there.
   *Cho.*—I'm so glad, &c.

## 238. Come, let us all go Down.

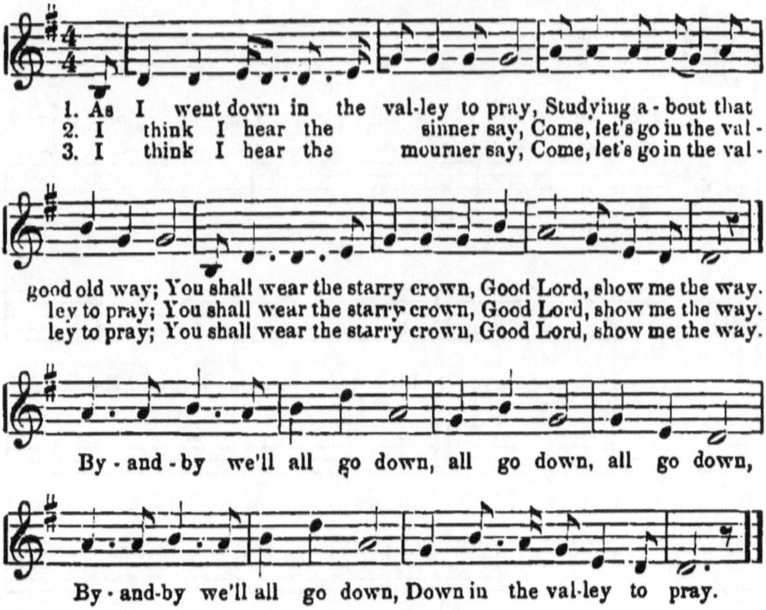

1. As I went down in the val-ley to pray, Studying a-bout that good old way; You shall wear the starry crown, Good Lord, show me the way.
2. I think I hear the sinner say, Come, let's go in the val-ley to pray; You shall wear the starry crown, Good Lord, show me the way.
3. I think I hear the mourner say, Come, let's go in the val-ley to pray; You shall wear the starry crown, Good Lord, show me the way.

By-and-by we'll all go down, all go down, all go down,
By-and-by we'll all go down, Down in the val-ley to pray.

## Zion's Children.

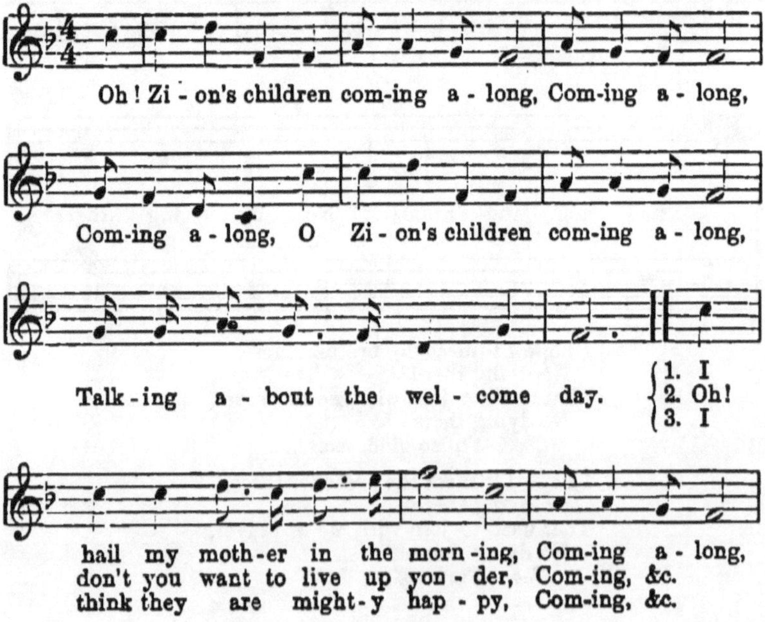

Oh! Zi-on's children com-ing a-long, Com-ing a-long,
Com-ing a-long, O Zi-on's children com-ing a-long,
Talk-ing a-bout the wel-come day.

1. I hail my moth-er in the morn-ing, Com-ing a-long,
2. Oh! don't you want to live up yon-der, Com-ing, &c.
3. I think they are might-y hap-py, Com-ing, &c.

## Oh! Holy Lord.

2. What a glorious morning that will be,
   Done with the sin and sorrow;
   Our friends and Jesus we will see,
   Done with the sin and sorrow.—*Cho.*

3. Oh shout, you Christians, you're gaining ground,
   Done with the sin and sorrow;
   We'll shout old Satan's kingdom down,
   Done with the sin and sorrow.—*Cho.*

4. I soon shall reach that golden shore,
   Done with the sin and sorrow;
   And sing the songs we sang before,
   Done with the sin and sorrow.—*Cho.*

## This Old Time Religion.

2. It will carry you home to heaven,
   It will carry you home to heaven,
   It will carry you home to heaven,
   It is good enough for me.
   *Cho.*—Oh, this old time religion, &c.

3. It brought me out of bondage, &c.
   *Cho.*—Oh, this old time religion, &c.

4. It is good when you are in trouble, &c.
   *Cho.*—Oh, this old time religion, &c.

## The Ten Virgins.

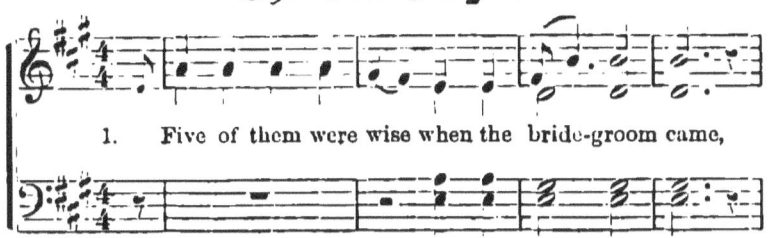

1. Five of them were wise when the bride-groom came,

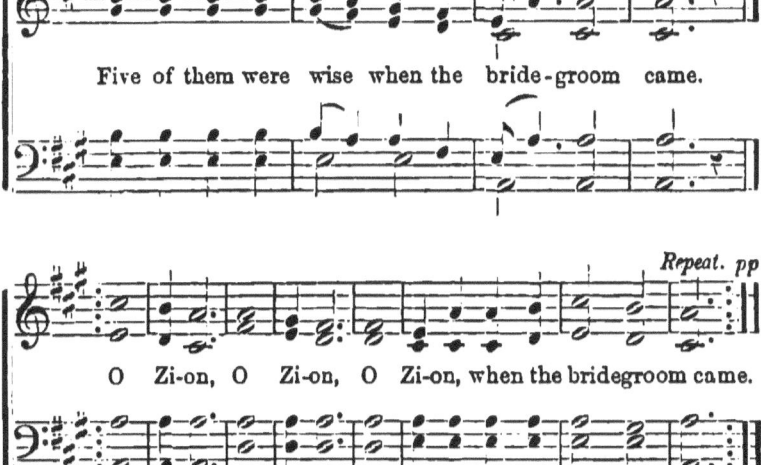

Five of them were wise when the bride-groom came.

O Zi-on, O Zi-on, O Zi-on, when the bridegroom came.

2. Five of them were foolish when the bridegroom came,
   Five of them were foolish when the bridegroom came.
   *Cho.*—O Zion, &c.

3. The wise they took oil when the bridegroom came,
   The wise they took oil when the bridegroom came.
   *Cho.*—O Zion, &c.

4. The foolish took no oil when the bridegroom came,
   The foolish took no oil when the bridegroom came.
   *Cho.*—O Zion, &c.

5. The foolish they kept knocking when the bridegroom came,
   The foolish they kept knocking when the bridegroom came.
   *Cho.*—O Zion, &c.

6. Depart, I never knew you, said the bridegroom, then,
   Depart, I never knew you, said the bridegroom, then.
   *Cho.*—O Zion, &c.

2. Then down came an angel,
Then down came an angel,
Then down came an angel,
And rolled away the stone.
Cho.—He arose, &c.

3. Then Mary she came weeping,
Then Mary she came weeping,
Then Mary she came weeping,
A looking for her Lord.
Cho.—He arose, &c.

## Save me, Lord, Save.

2. I called to my mother, my mother hearkened to me,
   And the last word I heard her say
   Was, Save me, Lord, save me,
   *Cho.*—And I wish that heav'n was a mine, &c.

3. I called to my sister, my sister hearkened to me, &c.
   *Cho.*—And I wish that heav'n was a mine, &c.

4. I called to my brother, my brother hearkened to me, &c.
   *Cho.*—And I wish that heav'n was a mine, &c.

## 244. Judgment will find you so.

2. The tallest tree in paradise,
    Judgment will find you so;
   The Christian calls the tree of life,
    Judgment will find you so.
     *Cho.*—Just as you live, &c.

3. Oh! Hallelujah to the Lamb,
    Judgment will find you so;
   The Lord is on the giving hand,
    Judgment will find you so.
     *Cho.*—Just as you live, &c.

# He's the Lily of the Valley. 245

2. What kind of shoes are those you wear,
   Oh! my Lord;
   That you can ride upon the air,
   Oh! my Lord.
   *Cho.*—He's the lily of the valley, &c.

3. These shoes I wear are gospel shoes,
   Oh! my Lord;
   And you can wear them if you choose,
   Oh! my Lord.
   *Cho.*—He's the lily of the valley, &c.

## Prepare us.

2. The man that loves to serve the Lord,
   When death shall shake this frame;
   He will receive his just reward,
   When death shall shake this frame.
   *Cho.*—Prepare me, &c.

3. Am I a soldier of the cross,
   When death shall shake this frame;
   Or must I count this soul as lost,
   When death shall shake this frame.
   *Cho.*—Prepare me, &c.

4. My soul is bound for that bright land,
   When death shall shake this frame;
   And there I'll meet that happy band,
   When death shall shake this frame.
   *Cho.*—Prepare me, &c.

## My Ship is on the Ocean.    247

2. I'm going to see the weeping Mary,
   I'm going away to see my Lord.
   *Cho.*—My ship, &c.

3. Oh! don't you want to live in that bright glory?
   Oh! don't you want to go to see my Lord?
   *Cho.*—My ship, &c.

## March On.

2. When Peter was preaching at the Pentecost,
   You shall gain the victory;
   He was endowed with the Holy Ghost,
   You shall gain the day.
   *Cho.*—March on, &c.

3. When Peter was fishing in the sea,
   You shall gain the victory;
   He dropped his net and followed me,
   You shall gain the day.
   *Cho.*—March on, &c.

4. King Jesus on the mountain top,
   You shall gain the victory;
   King Jesus speaks and the chariot stops,
   You shall gain the day.
   *Cho.*—March on, &c.

## Ride on, King Jesus.

Ride on, King Je - sus, No man can a hin-der me,

Ride on, King Je - sus, No man can a hinder me.

1. I was but young when I begun, No man can a hinder me, But

*D. C.*

now my race is almost done, No man can a hinder me.

2. King Jesus rides on a milk-white horse,
    No man can a hinder me;
  The river of Jordan he did cross,
    No man can a hinder me.
      *Cho.*—Ride on, &c.

3. If you want to find your way to God,
    No man can a hinder me;
  The gospel highway must be trod,
    No man can a hinder me.
      *Cho.*—Ride on, &c.

## These are my Father's Children.

These are my Father's children, These are my Father's children,

These are my Father's chil-dren, All.... in one band.

1. And I soon shall be done with the troubles of the world,

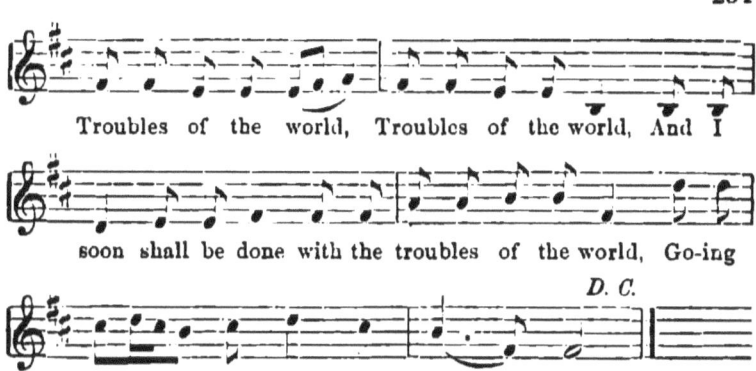

Troubles of the world, Troubles of the world, And I soon shall be done with the troubles of the world, Going home.... to live with God, Oh!

2. My brother's done with the troubles of the world, &c.
   *Cho.*—These are my Father's children, &c.

3. My sister's done with the troubles of the world, &c.
   *Cho.*—These are my Father's children, &c.

## Reign, Oh! Reign.

Reign, Oh! reign, O reign, my Saviour, Reign, Oh! reign, O reign, my Lord. 1. Takes an humble soul to join us in the service of the Lord, Takes an humble soul to join us in the army.

2. Here's a sinner come to join us in the service of the Lord,
   Here's a sinner come to join us in the army.
       *Cho.*—Reign, Oh! reign, &c.

3. Oh! ain't you glad you've joined us in the service of the Lord;
   Oh! ain't you glad you've joined us in the army.
       *Cho.*—Reign, Oh! reign, &c.

## Mary and Martha.

Jordan, Lord, Way over Jordan, Lord, To ring those charming bells.

2. The preacher and the elder's just gone 'long, &c.
   To ring those charming bells.
   *Cho.*—Crying, free grace, &c.
3. My father and mother's just gone 'long, &c.
   To ring those charming bells.
   *Cho.*—Crying, free grace, &c.
4. The Methodist and Baptist's just gone 'long, &c.
   To ring those charming bells.
   *Cho.*—Crying, free grace, &c.

## I ain't going to die no more.

Oh! ain't I glad, Oh! ain't I glad, Oh! ain't I glad, I ain't a going to die no more; 1. Going to meet those happy Christians sooner in the morning, Sooner in the morning, Sooner in the morning, Meet those happy Christians sooner in the morning, I ain't a going to die no more.

2. Going shouting home to glory sooner in the morning, &c.
   *Cho.*—Oh! ain't I glad, &c.
3. Going to wear the starry crown sooner in the morning, &c.
   *Cho.*—Oh! ain't I glad, &c.
4. We'll sing our troubles over sooner in the morning, &c.
   *Cho.*—Oh! ain't I glad, &c.

## Getting Ready to Die.

Get-ting read-y to die, Get-ting read-y to die, Getting read-y to die, O Zi-on, Zi-on,

1. When I set out, I was but young, Zi-on, Zi-on, But now my race is al-most run, Zi-on, Zi-on.

2. Religion's like a blooming rose, Zion, Zion,
And none but those that feel it knows, Zion, Zion.
*Cho.*—Getting ready to die, &c.

3. The Lord is waiting to receive, Zion, Zion,
If sinners only would believe, Zion, Zion.—*Chorus.*

4. All those who walk in Gospel shoes, Zion, Zion,
This faith in Christ they'll never lose, Zion, Zion.—*Chorus.*

## The General Roll.

I'll be there, I'll be there, Oh when the general roll is called, I'll be there.

1. O hal-le-lu-jah to the Lamb, The general roll is called, I'll be there; The Lord is on the giv-ing hand, The gen-eral roll is called, I'll be there.

2. Old Sa-tan told me not to pray, The general roll is called, I'll be there; He wants my soul at Judgment Day, The gen-eral roll is called, I'll be there.

## I'm Troubled in Mind.

[The person who furnished this song (Mrs. Brown of Nashville, formerly a slave), stated that she first heard it from her old father when she was a child. After he had been whipped he always went and sat upon a certain log near his cabin, and with the tears streaming down his cheeks, sang this song with so much pathos that few could listen without weeping from sympathy: and even his cruel oppressors were not wholly unmoved.]

I'm troubled, I'm troubled, I'm troubled in mind, If Jesus don't

help me, I sure-ly will die. 1. O Jesus, my Saviour, on

thee I'll depend, When troubles are near me, you'll be my true friend.

2. When ladened with trouble and burdened with grief,
To Jesus in secret I'll go for relief.
*Cho.*—I'm troubled, &c.

3. In dark days of bondage to Jesus I prayed,
To help me to bear it, and he gave me his aid.
*Cho.*—I'm troubled, &c.

## I'm going to Live with Jesus.

1. I'm going to live with Je-sus, A soldier of the Ju-bi-lee, I'm
2. I've start-ed out for heav-en, A soldier of the Ju-bi-lee, I've
3. I know I love my Je-sus, A soldier of the Ju-bi-lee, I

going to live with Je-sus, A sol-dier of the cross.
start-ed out for heav-en, A sol-dier of the cross.
know I love my Je-sus, A sol-dier of the cross.

Oh! when you get there remember me, A soldier of the Jubilee, Oh!

when you get there remember me. A sol-dier of the cross.

## Oh! let me get up.

1. Oh! just let me get up in the house of God, Just let me get up in the house of God, Just let me get up in the house of God, And I'll nev-er turn back a-ny more. No more, no more, why thank God al-might-y, No more, no more, I'll nev-er turn back a-ny more.

2. Oh! just let me get on my long white robe, &c.
3. Oh! just let me get on my starry crown, &c.
4. Oh! just let me get on my golden shoes, &c.
5. Oh! the music in the heaven, and it sounds so sweet, &c.

## Go, chain the Lion down.

Go, chain the li-on down, Go, chain the li-on down, Go, chain the li-on down, Be-fore the heav'n doors close. 1. Do you see that good old sis-ter, Come a wagging up the hill so slow, She wants to get to heav'n in due time. Be-fore the heav'n doors close.

D. C.

2. Do you see the good old Christians? &c.
3. Do you see the good old preachers? &c.

# When Moses smote the Water.

2. O Christians ain't you glad
   You've left that sinful army?
   O Christians ain't you glad
   The sea gave away?
   *Cho.*—When Moses smote, &c.

3. O brothers ain't you glad
   You've left that sinful army?
   O brothers ain't you glad
   The sea gave away?
   *Cho.*—When Moses smote, &c.

## Oh! Sinner Man.

2. Though days be dark, and nights be long,
   Which way are you going?
   We'll shout and sing till we get home,
   Which way are you going?
   *Cho.*—Oh! sinner, &c.

3. 'Twas just about the break of day,
   Which way are you going?
   My sins forgiven and soul set free,
   Which way are you going?
   *Cho.*—Oh! sinner, &c.

## My good Lord's been here. 259

2. O sinners, where were you, &c.
   *Cho.*—My good Lord's been here, &c.

3. O Christians, where were you, &c.
   *Cho.*—My good Lord's been here, &c.

4. O mourners, where were you, &c.
   *Cho.*—My good Lord's been here, &c.

## 260. A little more Faith in Jesus.

2.
I tell you now as I told you before,
  A little more faith in Jesus,
To the promised land I'm bound to go,
  A little more faith in Jesus.
    *Cho.*—All I want, &c.

3.
Oh! Hallelujah to the Lamb,
  A little more faith in Jesus,
The Lord is on the giving hand,
  A little more faith in Jesus.
    *Cho.*—All I want, &c.

4.
I do believe without a doubt,
  A little more faith in Jesus,
That Christians have a right to shout,
  A little more faith in Jesus.
    *Cho.*—All I want, &c.

5.
Shout, you children, shout, you're free,
  A little more faith in Jesus,
For Christ has bought this liberty,
  A little more faith in Jesus.
    *Cho.*—All I want, &c.

# Did not old Pharaoh get lost? 261

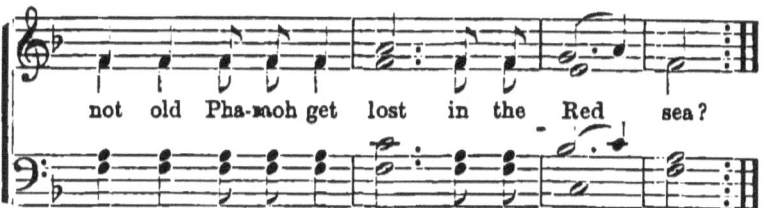

2. Joseph, by his false brethren sold,
   God raised above them all ;
To Hannah's child the Lord foretold
   How Eli's house should fall.
    *Cho.*—Did not old Pharaoh, &c.

3. The Lord said unto Moses,
   Go unto Pharaoh now,
For I have hardened Pharaoh's heart,
   To me he will not bow.
    *Cho.*—Did not old Pharaoh, &c.

4. Then Moses and Aaron,
   To Pharaoh did go,
Thus says the God of Israel,
   Let my people go.
    *Cho.*—Did not old Pharaoh, &c.

5. Old Pharaoh said who is the Lord,
   That I should Him obey?
His name it is Jehovah,
   For he hears his people pray.
    *Cho.*—Did not old Pharaoh, &c.

6. Then Moses numbered Israel,
   Through all the land abroad,
Saying, children, do not murmur,
   But hear the word of God.
    *Cho.*—Did not old Pharaoh, &c.

7. Hark ! hear the children murmur,
   They cried aloud for bread,
Down came the hidden manna,
   The hungry soldiers fed.
    *Cho.*—Did not old Pharaoh, &c.

8. Then Moses said to Israel,
   As they stood along the shore,
Your enemies you see to-day,
   You will never see no more.
    *Cho.*—Did not old Pharaoh, &c.

9. Then down came raging Pharaoh,
   That you may plainly see,
Old Pharaoh and his host,
   Got lost in the Red Sea.
    *Cho.*—Did not old Pharaoh, &c.

10. Then men, and women, and children
    To Moses they did flock ;
They cried aloud for water,
    And Moses smote the rock.
     *Cho.*—Did not old Pharaoh, &c.

11. And the Lord spoke to Moses,
    From Sinai's smoking top,
Saying, Moses, lead the people,
    Till I shall bid you stop.
     *Cho.*—Did not old Pharaoh, &c.

262 Wrestling Jacob.

# Love-feast in Heaven.

2 Old Satan told me not to pray, &c.
He wants my soul at the Judgment-day, &c.

3 Oh, brethren, and sisters, how do you do, &c.
And does your love continue true, &c.

4 Oh, brethren, brethren, how do you know, &c.
Because my Jesus told me so, &c.

## When shall I get there. 265

2 John and Peter ran to see,
  When shall I get there?
 But Christ had gone to Galilee,
  When shall I get there?

3 Paul and Silas bound in jail,
  When shall I get there?
 They sang and prayed both night and day,
  When shall I get there?

4 I'm bred and born a Methodist,
  When shall I get there?
 I carry the witness in my breast,
  When shall I get there?

2 Those angels wings are tipped with gold, &c.
That brought glad tidings to my soul, &c.

3 My father says it is the best, &c.
To live and die a Methodist, &c.

4 I'm a Methodist bred and a Methodist born, &c.
And when I'm dead there's a Methodist gone, &c.

## Farewell, my Brother.

Farewell, my brother,* farewell for-ev-er, Fare you well, my broth-er, now, For I am go-ing home. Oh good-bye, good-bye, For I am bound to leave you, Oh good-bye, good-bye, for I am going home.

*After Da Capo sing this:*
Shake hands, shake hands, for I am bound to leave you,
Oh, shake hands, &c.

\* *Or Sister.*

## Inching along.

[Attention is called to the appropriateness of the melody for the expression of these singular words. It is all embraced within the first three tones of the scale, and thus may be said to be itself not more than an inch long.]

2 The Lord is coming to take us home,
   Jesus will come by'nd-bye.
   And then our work will soon be done,
   Jesus will come by'nd-bye.

3 Trials and troubles are on the way,
   Jesus will come by'nd-bye.
   But we must watch and always pray,
   Jesus will come by'nd-bye.

4 We'll inch and inch and inch along,
   Jesus will come by'nd-bye.
   And inch and inch till we get home,
   Jesus will come by'nd-bye.

# I ain't got weary yet. 269

2 Been praying for the mourner so long, &c.
3 Been going to the sitting-up so long, &c.

## Run to Jesus.

[This song was given to the Jubilee Singers by Hon. FREDERICK DOUGLASS, at Washington, D. C., with the interesting statement, that it first suggested to him the thought of escaping from slavery.]

Run to Je - sus, shun the dan - ger, I

don't ex - pect to stay much long - er here. 1. He will

be our dear-est friend, And will help us to the end. I

don't ex-pect to stay much long - er here. Run to Je - sus,

shun the dan - ger, I don't ex-pect to stay much long-er here.

2 Oh, I thought I heard them say,
There were lions in the way.
   I don't expect, etc.

3 Many mansions there will be,
One for you and one for me.
   I don't expect, etc.

# Angels waiting at the Door.

1. My sister's took her flight and gone home, And the
2. She has laid down her cross and gone home, And, &c.
3. She has taken up her crown and gone home, And, &c.

an-gel's wait-ing at the door. My sis-ter's took her flight and gone home, And the angels waiting at the door.

Tell all my fa-ther's children, Don't you grieve for me;

Tell all my fa-ther's children, Don't you grieve for me.

## Keep your Lamps trimmed.

Keep your lamps trimmed and a-burning, Keep your lamps trimmed and a-

burning, Keep your lamps trimm'd and a-burning, For this world's almost done.

Brothers, don't grow wea-ry, Brothers, don't grow wea-ry,
Preachers, &c.

Brothers, don't grow wea-ry, For this world's al-most done.

Keep your lamps trimmed and a-burning, Keep your lamps trimmed and a-

burning, Keep your lamps trimm'd and a-burning, For this world's almost done.

'Tis re-lig-ion makes us hap-py, 'Tis re-lig-ion makes us
We are climbing Ja-cob's lad-der, &c.
Ev-ery round goes higher and higher, &c.

hap-py, 'Tis religion, makes us happy, For this world's almost done.

# INDEX TO MUSIC.

PREFACE TO THE MUSIC.................................................. 205

| | PAGE | | PAGE |
|---|---|---|---|
| A little more faith in Jesus | 260 | Mary and Martha | 252 |
| Angels waiting at the door | 271 | My good Lord's been here | 259 |
| Been a-listening | 226 | My Ship is on the Ocean | 247 |
| Children, you'll be called on | 222 | My Way's cloudy | 249 |
| Children, we all shall be free | 212 | Nobody knows the Trouble I see | 207 |
| Come, let us all go down | 238 | Oh! holy Lord | 239 |
| Did not old Pharaoh get lost? | 261 | Old Ship of Zion | 234 |
| Didn't my Lord deliver Daniel | 216 | O! let me get up | 256 |
| Farewell, my brother | 264 | O, Redeemed | 210 |
| From every Grave-yard | 211 | O! Sinner Man | 258 |
| Getting ready to die | 254 | Prepare us | 246 |
| Give me Jesus | 222 | Reign, O reign | 251 |
| Go down, Moses | 224 | Ride on, King Jesus | 250 |
| Go, chain the Lion down | 256 | Rise, Mourners | 218 |
| Gwine to ride up in the Chariot | 220 | Roll, Jordan, roll | 213 |
| He arose | 242 | Room enough | 209 |
| He's the Lily of the Valley | 245 | Run to Jesus | 270 |
| He's the Lord of Lords | 230 | Save me, Lord, save me | 243 |
| I ain't going to die no more | 253 | Shine, shine | 233 |
| I ain't got weary yet | 269 | Steal away | 229 |
| I'll hear the Trumpet sound | 218 | Swing low, sweet Chariot | 208 |
| I'm a-rolling | 215 | The General Roll | 254 |
| I'm a-travelling to the Grave | 228 | The Gospel Train | 232 |
| I'm going to live with Jesus | 255 | The Rocks and the Mountains | 223 |
| I'm so glad | 237 | These are my Father's Children | 250 |
| I'm troubled in Mind | 255 | There's a Meeting here to-night | 266 |
| Inching along | 268 | The Ten Virgins | 241 |
| In the River of Jordan | 235 | This Old Time Religion | 240 |
| I've just come from the Fountain | 219 | Turn back Pharaoh's Army | 214 |
| Judgment-day is rolling round | 231 | We'll die in the Field | 221 |
| Judgment will find you so | 244 | We'll stand the Storm | 236 |
| Keep me from sinking down | 227 | When Moses smote the Waters | 257 |
| Keep your lamps trimmed and burning | 272 | When shall I get there | 265 |
| Love-feast in Heaven | 264 | Westling Jacob | 262 |
| Many Thousand gone | 228 | Zion's Children | 238 |
| March on | 248 | | |

# THE AMERICAN MISSIONARY ASSOCIATION'S
# WORK IN THE SOUTH,

is represented, in Christian Schools and in Churches, as follows:—

## CHARTERED INSTITUTIONS.

Hampton Normal and Agricultural Institute, Hampton, Virginia.—Number of pupils, 240. Boarding accommodations for 150 students.
Berea College, Berea, Ky.—Number of pupils, 287. Boarding accommodations for 200 students.
Fisk University, Nashville, Tenn.—Number of pupils, 390. Boarding accommodations for 100 students.
Atlanta University, Atlanta, Ga.—Number of pupils, 197. Boarding accommodations for 150 students.
Talladega College, Talladega, Ala.—Number of pupils, 198. Boarding accommodations for 100 students.
Tougaloo University, Tougaloo, Miss.—Number of pupils, 327. Boarding Accommodations for 100 students.
Straight University, New Orleans, La.—Number of pupils, 266. Boarding accommodations for 30 students.

## OTHER INSTITUTIONS.

| | |
|---|---|
| Williston Academy, Wilmington, N. C. | Lincoln School, Marion, Ala. |
| Avery Institute, Charleston, S. C. | Emerson Institute, Mobile, Ala. |
| Brewer Normal School, Greenwood, S.C. | Swayne School, Montgomery, Ala |
| Normal School, Andersonville, Ga. | Burrell School, Selma, Ala. |
| Storrs School, Atlanta, Ga. | Howard School, Chattanooga, Tenn. |
| Lewis High School, Macon, Ga. | La Moyne School, Memphis, Tenn. |
| Beach Institute, Savannah, Ga. | Normal School, Lexington, Ky. |
| Trinity School, Athens, Ala. | Union Academy, Columbus, Miss. |

Barnes Institute, Galveston, Texas.

Total number of pupils enrolled, 8,978. Classified: Theological, 76; Medical, 12; Law, 15; Collegiate, 46; Collegiate Preparatory, 231; Normal, 1,392; Grammar, 1,530; Intermediate, 2,452; Primary, 3,292. Studying in two grades, 18.

The estimated number of pupils taught in 1874, by teachers who had been educated in the schools of the Association, was 64,000.

## CHURCHES.

Number of Churches, 54; Church Members, 3,277; Number of Scholars in Church and Mission Sunday-schools, 9,605.
Number of Ministers, Missionaries, and Teachers, for 1874, 256.

E. M. CRAVATH, *Field Secretary.*

Rooms of the A. M. A., 56 Reade Street,

**NEW YORK.**

www.ingramcontent.com/pod-product-compliance
Lightning Source LLC
Chambersburg PA
CBHW031336230426
43670CB00006B/351